MOUNTAIN BIKE GUIDE

Mountain Bike Guide Midlands

by

Dave Taylor

Acknowledgements

This guide could not have been completed without the help and support of my wife, Carol. Without her encouragement the book would probably have sunk without trace, most likely in an extremely muddy field somewhere in Warwickshire! I thank my wife also for being general navigator, support vehicle driver, and for demonstrating on Dumbleton Hill how best to do a face plant (thanks also due to Specialized for producing such good helmets!). My wife also took many of the photographs in the book, proofread the MS and most importantly of all, was my companion on many of the routes. She also makes the best homemade soup in the world – just what you need after a hard day in the saddle!

Thanks are also due to the Forestry Commission and in particular Jerry Gissop and friends at Marches Forest District, Ludlow, for all the help and support they have given. I hope the Forestry Commission continue to show such an enlightened attitude towards mountain bikers.

I am also most grateful to Mr Williams of Vron Farm, Bucknell for allowing the use of a short section of private track across his land where it enters Bucknell Wood. Please keep to this permissive track, close all gates and do not spoil it for others.

Lastly, thanks to all those mountain bikers I met whilst out doing these routes. Their friendliness and enthusiasm helped provide me with the inspiration to complete this guide.

The publishers acknowledge editorial and production supervision by Susan Hodgkiss.

CONTENTS

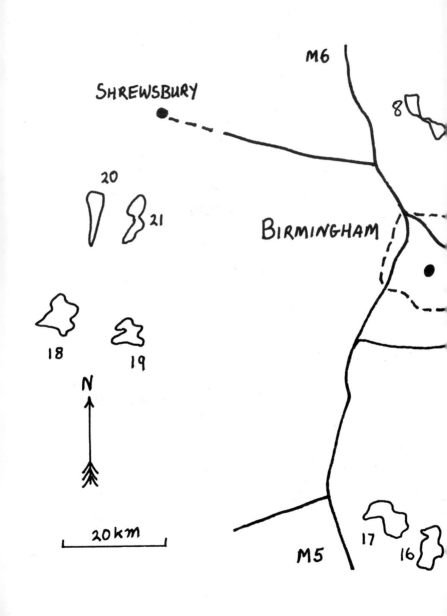

INTRODUCTION

At first sight, it might appear that a book entitled 'Mountain Bike Guide – Midlands' could be a contradiction in terms. True, there are few mountains in the Midlands, but there are many hills and the area is crisscrossed by a network of ancient tracks, bridleways, disused county roads, canals and pretty country lanes. All of these, when carefully linked together, make for very interesting and enjoyable on and off road biking.

Recent years have seen an explosion in the popularity of mountain biking, if retail sales of bikes are any indication. In reality the author suspects that, although many mountain bikes are sold each year, a significant number rarely, if ever, see a grassy bridleway, woodland track or rocky hill path! Where mountain bikes are used off road in appreciable numbers, such as in areas like the Lake District or the Dales, they are perceived as yet another threat to an already over-stressed environment. One of the aims of this book is to redress the balance somewhat. This guide illustrates that there is plenty of mountain biking fun to be had in other areas of the country, which can be just as challenging in its own right.

Many owners of mountain bikes, particularly those new to the sport, do not necessarily relish the challenge of carrying a bike to the top of a 3000ft mountain, but would appreciate simple, easy to follow and reliable descriptions of where to ride off road, legally. This book will provide some guidance for such folk, although it would be a mistake to assume that all the routes in this book are easy! In any case, given the wrong conditions even the easiest looking route can become a real challenge.

The routes described vary greatly in style and difficulty. Some would make an ideal day out for a family group, whilst the more experienced hammerhead might prefer to thrash around in an afternoon. Other routes are perhaps best savoured on a fine summer's evening, when there are fewer people about and the pubs are more likely to be open. Whatever type of mountain biker you are, I am sure that you will find that these routes will prove interesting and enjoyable. Mountain biking should not be all high-tech and glitzy, it should also be about appreciating the countryside, with a little bit of fitness and a lot of fun.

ENVIRONMENT

One of my concerns as the author of this guide, has been its potential effect on the environment. Fortunately, unlike the more popular areas such as the Lake District, mountain biking is not yet generally perceived to be a great problem in the Midlands. It is hoped that, whilst it is the intention to encourage mountain biking in the area, this guide will not create problems of conflict of interest.

In spite of the fact that the area contains such large conurbations as Birmingham, Leicester and Coventry, the rural districts between are very quiet and as yet, largely unexplored by mountain bikes. Roadies have long been aware of the potential for riding in this area, on quiet lanes which are largely deserted, even on a Sunday afternoon. True, it would be misleading to try to suggest that it is possible to devise completely off road routes in the area; but by linking bridleways and tracks with small country lanes, it is easy to create interesting routes.

Herein, however, lies a slight problem. The area is characterised by quite intensive farming and although bridleways may exist on the Ordnance Survey map, the reality is often different on the ground. The continued existence of a bridleway seems to depend to a great extent on whether or not there is a history of horse riding in the area. Where the latter is not the case, the bridleway may well have been downgraded to a footpath or lost altogether. Even where the bridleway still exists, the amount of use it gets determines whether it is possible to ride it or not. Whatever the case, the continued use of such bridleways by mountain bikers will only be accepted by local farmers and the public if they can be persuaded that mountain bikers are essentially jolly decent, country loving folk, at least in public! To this end, the Mountain Bike Club have issued an Off Road Code and I urge all to follow it, for the sake of the future of the sport.

The Off Road Code

- Only ride where you know you have a legal right.
- Always give way to horses and pedestrians.
- Avoid animals and crops.
- Take all litter with you.
- Leave all gates as found.
- Keep the noise down.
- Don't get annoyed with anyone, it never solves problems.
- Always try to be self-sufficient, for you and your bike.
- Never create a fire hazard.

In addition to this, there is of course the Country Code, issued by the Countryside Commission

The Country Code

- Enjoy the countryside and respect its life and work.
- Guard against the risk of fire.
- Fasten all gates.
- Keep your dogs under close control.
- Keep to public rights of way across farmland.
- Use gates and stiles to cross fences, hedges and walls.
- Leave livestock, crops and machinery alone.
- Take your litter home.
- Help keep all water clean.
- Protect wildlife, plants and trees.
- Take special care on country roads.
- Make no unnecessary noise.

All of the above begs the question, what actually is a right of way?

RIGHTS OF WAY

The future of mountain biking is very much in the hands of those who ride mountain bikes. The whole ethos associated with mountain biking is one of fun, freedom and adventure. Although rules seem to be the antipathy of the sport, these codes need to be followed. It is very easy to be romantic about the rural landscape. In reality, particularly in the Midlands, the countryside is one big factory, albeit a very pretty one on occasions. Landowners and farmers who view the countryside as a business do not take kindly to the public, whether on foot, horse or bike, causing disruption and possibly threatening their livelihood. It is essential, therefore, to be aware of where you may ride legally.

There are four types of right of way as detailed on the OS maps, of which three are open to off road riding.

Public Footpath – this is a right of way on foot only. **Mountain bikers do not have a right of way on footpaths**. If you ride your bike onto a footpath you are committing a civil offence and as such could be sued by the landowner for damage to property. Best advice is, keep off – no go area!

Bridleways – These are open to the public on foot, on horseback and on bicycle, provided that cyclists give way to horses and pedestrians. It is important to remember that cyclists have only had this right since 1968 and are therefore comparative newcomers, so smile nicely and give way to any walkers or horses that you see. Bridleways are usually marked by a blue waymarker, although not all local councils are as careful as they might be and, occasionally, you may only see yellow footpath markers.

BOATS – or Byways Open to All Traffic. As the classification implies, these are open to all vehicles as well as pedestrians, horses and cyclists. Unfortunately, a minority of users of four-wheel drive vehicles and motor-cycles have succeeded in making a real mess of some of these excellent tracks and even the adjoining land, much to the annoyance of the landowners.

RUPPS – These are Roads Used as Public Paths. Take care with these! In the Midlands at least, these have a nasty habit of no longer existing on the ground, or have been downgraded to the status of a footpath. Where they do exist, many local councils are now in the process of reclassifying these to BOATS or Bridleways.

In addition to the four types of rights of way there are also:

Unclassified County Roads – These very minor roads are often unsurfaced and are usually not maintained. Whilst not strictly 'off road' as such, they can range in appearance from superb walled tracks to little more than linear depressions in the ground. In effect they have the same status as a byway, but on the map it may not be clear whether they are a right of way or a private track. Consultation with the definitive map held by the Highways department of the County Council will usually clarify.

Canal towpaths – The industrial heritage of the Midlands has bequeathed an extensive network of canals and their associated towpaths. With the increase in leisure activities in general, many of these towpaths are now in excellent condition, but it is important to remember that these paths are **not** public rights of way. British Waterways, who own most of the canal network, do allow use of the towpaths by cyclists, subject to certain restrictions. Firstly, in order to use the path it is necessary to obtain and subsequently display, a permit from British Waterways. This, at present, costs around £3 for a year and covers a fairly large area. The address for the Midlands regional office is included in the appendix at the back of this guide. Secondly, certain stretches of canal may not be available to cyclists due to, for example, the condition of the path or the towpath coinciding with a public footpath. That said, the canal system is very extensive and whilst it may not present the most challenging of off road riding, it is often very scenic. Take care, however! Towpaths can be rather narrow in places and soft at the edges. Look out for low bridges and obstructions on the path. Keep your speed down and be aware, otherwise you might just take an unexpected dip in the murky waters.

Forest Tracks – A great deal of woodland is managed by the Forestry Commission. In the past, access has been difficult, but recently the Commission has shown a more enlightened attitude and opened up areas of their land for leisure activities, initially for walkers. All tracks on Forestry Commission land are private, unless they coincide with recognised rights of way. However, in many areas, the Commission have indicated that they are happy for bikers to use any of the gravel tracks within their forests. This should always be checked with the local office, as restrictions may be introduced at any time. If you do use the forestry tracks, have consideration for others.

There is a strong urge to 'let rip' on these tracks and as a consequence terrify the local Sunday afternoon trippers! This is a sure way to get mountain bikers banned from the forest and has already created problems in certain areas; for example, Cannock Chase, which is much frequented by the local populace and in recent years has also become very popular with bikers. To alleviate problems of this nature, the Forestry Commission are now making available areas specifically aimed at mountain bikers. A good example of this is Hopton Wood in Shropshire, which has waymarked trails of varying difficulty. Facilities of this kind can be expected only if mountain bikers show that they are responsible enjoyers of the countryside.

EQUIPMENT

Although this guide shows that it is perfectly possible to bike off road in the Midlands and escape the hassle of modern life, an off road experience in Northamptonshire is hardly likely to have the same degree of seriousness as a day out on Helvellyn. There are, however, a few points about equipment that are relevant, regardless of where you are biking.

The Bike

The type of mountain bike you prefer to ride is very much a personal choice. There is a great deal of hype surrounding mountain biking technology that, for most people, is pretty irrelevant, except when it comes to 'pose value'! Choose the best bike you can afford, but remember what you are going to put it through. A well-built chromoly bike is probably a more sensible choice than the latest Aluminium and Titanium technology, bedecked with numerous widgets. That said, there are a few devices that I have found particularly helpful when biking in the Midlands. As you might expect, mud can be more than a slight problem in this part of the country! Personally, I detest mudguards, but I have found the detachable Crud Catcher an excellent insurance against those unpleasant 'black outs' caused by flying mud from the front wheel when on a rapid descent. An equally useful device is the Crud Claw, which is excellent at scraping mud and bits of arable field out of the rear mech.

11

Clothing and Safety

Again, this is a very personal matter and there is more than enough advice in the magazines and books on what should be worn. In the event of a crash, however, what you are wearing could have an important effect on how well you survive! One item that is essential, is a helmet. Find one that fits and **use it!** This may seem a pain at first, and helmets are not cheap, but consider the consequences of a bad crash without one. Having seen how effective they are in practice, I have no doubt about their value. Also, consider investing in a pair of gloves, they will make the ride more comfortable and protect your hands in the event of a fall. Glasses too, are a good idea. Not only do they look cool, they also keep nasties like bugs, mud and twigs out of your eyes. Whilst on the subject of safety, it is perhaps a good idea to carry a small first aid kit. This might include nothing more than a few plasters, a roll of bandage, lint, and a pair of scissors, but you never know when it might be needed!

Tools

Many books have been written regarding the maintenance and repair of bikes and I would not presume to improve on their advice. A basic tool kit can, however, prevent a pleasant day out from degenerating into farce. At a minimum the kit should include:– a universal spanner, Allen keys, small screwdriver, tyre levers, pump, spare tube and puncture repair kit. The last three items I have found absolutely essential. A particular problem in the Midlands is the prevalence of hedges which, after they have been trimmed, leave nice little sharp thorns all over the track. Expect puncture repairs to be the norm!

THE ROUTES

Each route is accompanied by a map, summary, details of the route, an introduction and a description. I have tried to indicate places of interest en-route within the introduction and occasionally in the description. A few words of explanation are required regarding the route details.

Grade – I have found it particularly difficult to grade these routes. A descriptive grade can only be subjective at the best of times and is always dependent on many factors. In trying to grade these routes I have assumed the following:

– that the rider is of very average fitness; that is, they are neither a couch potato nor a health and fitness freak given to 100km bike rides.

– that the surface conditions are reasonably good, i.e. not completely water-logged! This was certainly not the case during the autumn and winter of 92/93. The rideability of some of the routes is severely affected by the surface conditions. In very wet conditions it becomes impossible to even push a bike across ploughed fields, let alone ride it. I have assumed a fairly typical(?) British summer of sunshine and showers, hence you should expect quite boggy bits in the woods. Less than ideal conditions could increase the difficulty considerably.

The grades are specific to the area – assuming good surface conditions, many of these routes would probably be graded as easy or moderate on a national basis, if only because the hills are of modest size. This would be of little help and could be misleading, as the difficulty of these routes is frequently dependent upon the state of the surface. I have therefore used a subjective system of grading similar to that used in rock climbing. Each grade is severely affected by personal fitness, surface conditions and should be taken with a large bucket of salt!

Easy – Few difficulties, probably uses canal towpaths and a reasonable proportion of country lanes, only crosses fields on good tracks, little or no hill climbing.

Moderate – Some difficulties may be encountered, perhaps due to small hill climbs, or soft woodland tracks and occasional poor, field edge bridleways.

Difficult – Expect some difficulties with bridleways across arable fields, soft woodland tracks, or a significant hill climb.

Very difficult – Definitely significant hill climbs, may also have sections on soft woodland tracks or across arable fields on ill-defined tracks.

Severe – Lots of hill climbing with sections across arable fields and ill-defined tracks.

Very severe – Totally flat countryside, non-existent tracks across ploughed fields, after a month of torrential rain. Fortunately, there are no such routes in this guide!

Time – The times can only be approximate, bearing in mind the factors described above. I have not allowed any time for cream teas, quick pints, jam butties, photos or puncture repairs!

Distance – I have tried to indicate the approximate proportion of on and off road riding. A minimum requirement when researching the routes was that each route should be at least 50% off road. Except for one route, Broadway, this criterion has been more than met. A second requirement was that any road riding should be on as few class A or B roads as possible. The vast majority of the roads used in these routes are in fact small, little used country lanes, with only the occasional use of a B road and, very rarely, an A road.

MAPS

As will be evident from the sketch-maps for each route, I am not, by any stretch of the imagination, an expert cartographer. Each map is intended only as guidance to support the route description. I would strongly recommend that the relevant Ordnance Survey map for the area be referred to for more information – the ideal procedure is to trace the route on the OS map before setting out, possibly marking it off with a highlighter.

The best map to use (aside from the 1:10 000 definitive maps held by the County Councils) is the Pathfinder 1:25 000 series. Unfortunately, the area covered by this guide is so large that the cost of buying all the required

Pathfinders would be prohibitive! However, armed with this guide book and the relevant 1:50 000 Landranger maps, you should encounter no route finding problems. The complete list of required maps is as follows:

127   Stafford, Telford & surrounding area
128   Derby & Burton upon Trent area
129   Nottingham & Loughborough area
137   Ludlow, Wenlock Edge & surrounding area
140   Leicester & Coventry area
141   Kettering, Corby & surrounding area
150   Worcester, The Malverns & surrounding area
151   Stratford-upon-Avon & surrounding area
152   Northampton & Milton Keynes area

LINKING ROUTES

Although some of the routes detailed in this guide are of fairly modest length, it is quite possible to combine routes to produce more demanding excursions, which might appeal to the more committed biker. This is particularly true of the routes in Shropshire and East Leicestershire. Here are some suggested combinations the reader might like to try.

Leicestershire – there is a wealth of old unclassified county roads and bridleways in the eastern half of this county and there are many variations possible here. For example, it would be possible to combine the Burrough Hill route with Rolleston and Quenby. Starting at Melton Mowbray, follow the Burrough Hill route to Tilton on the Hill, and then take the small lanes and field roads via Skeffington to Rolleston. Here you follow the Rolleston route, returning via Rolleston and a green lane to Billesdon, and then on to the Quenby route. Continue around this to Marefield and then return to Melton Mowbray as per the Burrough Hill route – Total distance about 75 km, at least 45 km of which would be off road.

Shropshire also offers many possibilities for extending routes. As is detailed in the route description, there are many variations possible around the Long Mynd. For example, it is possible to link this route to Hope Bowdler by starting at Church Stretton and taking the bridleway over Hope Bowdler Hill

15

to Willstone. Follow the Hope Bowdler route around The Lawley, and then cross over the valley to All Stretton and up onto the Mynd. The Portway can now be followed down to Plowden and the return to Church Stretton made via Hamperley and Little Stretton – Total distance about 40 km, about half off road depending on the exact route taken. Alternatively, it is possible to link the Hope Bowdler route with the bridleway which extends along much of the length of Wenlock Edge. This would produce a route of about 35 km, of which 20 km would be off road.

For those feeling really super fit, Shropshire County Council have now produced a mega-route called The Jack Mytton Way. This long distance bridleway, named after an 18th century equestrian-loving local eccentric(!), runs for over 70 miles and is available to mountain bikers and walkers, as well as horseriders. The route stretches from Billingsley in the east of the county, via Wenlock Edge, the Long Mynd and Offa's Dyke to finish at Llanfair Waterdine in the west. The route uses a combination of existing bridleways, tracks and lanes, together with some permissive sections. Information about this excellent route, together with an accommodation list, can be obtained from Shropshire County Council Leisure Services Department (address in the appendix).

KEY TO SKETCHMAP

Bridleway, usually a single track.

Bridleway, BOAT, RUPP, unclassified county road, usually a double track.

Metalled road, often through parkland and sometimes gated.

Metalled road.

Stream or river.

Railway line.

Trees.

Bridge.

Buildings.

Church.

Battlefield site.

Deserted village.

Trig point and height in metres.

Windmill.

Site of ancient fort or castle.

17

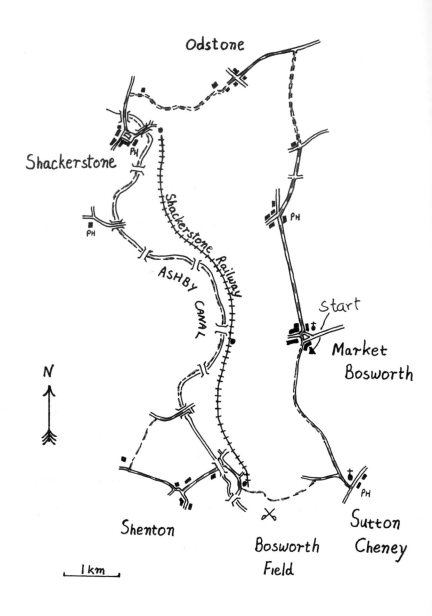

Odstone

Shackerstone

PH

Shackerstone Railway

ASHBY CANAL

N

Start

Market
Bosworth

Shenton

Bosworth
Field

Sutton
Cheney

PH

1 km

LEICESTERSHIRE

1. Market Bosworth and The Ashby Canal

Route Summary
Market Bosworth, Sutton Cheney, Bosworth Field, Shenton, Ashby Canal, Shackerstone, Odstone, Market Bosworth.

Details
Grade – easy.
Time – 2½ hours.
Distance – 27km
         off road – 15km
         on road – 12km
Terrain – farm land and canal towpaths.
Surface – easy towpaths, generally good farm tracks.
Start Grid Reference – SK 406030.
Maps – Leicester & Coventry area L140.

Introduction
This route, situated in almost the very centre of England, is possibly the easiest in the book. For that reason it is an ideal trip for those new to off road riding, families or those who just want to enjoy a quiet evening's ride. The landscape in these parts is generally flat, with occasional bumps to make things more interesting. Although there are bridleways in the area, these are often too widely spaced to make a reasonable off road route. However, by linking together small lanes, gated roads, canal towpaths and sections of bridleways it is possible to produce an easy but attractive route which is ideal for taking in the sights of an area rich in history, and well-suited for a lazy summer's afternoon or evening!

    The route is based around the very attractive small town of Market

Bosworth and passes through the battlefield site of Bosworth Field. The latter saw the end of the Plantagenet dynasty of Richard III and the rise of the Tudors in a scurrilous campaign in 1485. The treachery that brought the downfall of King Richard is still felt today and is marked by a plaque in St James church, Sutton Cheney, 'Remember before God Richard III King of England and those who fell at Bosworth Field having kept faith 22 August 1485'. The site is well worth a visit. The route also makes extensive use of the Ashby canal, a blind tributary of the Coventry canal. This has recently been renovated and the track is now in excellent condition, with seats and even picnic tables at intervals. It must be stressed that **bikes do not have a right of way** on the canal towpath, but are allowed to use the path upon the purchase of a permit, about £3 a year. The address to write to is included in the appendix.

Route Description

The route starts in the centre of Market Bosworth and goes due south past the Black Horse pub and some fine old half-timbered houses. Follow a lane signposted 'Sutton Cheney – Gated Road' to the gate and then down a delightful lane bordering Bosworth Park. Although this is a road it is more used by cattle than cars, so watch out for the cow pats! After passing through a second gate carry on up a slight hill to Sutton Cheney. This is an interesting little village with a couple of pubs and the old Almshouse tea rooms situated next to the Church of St James. It was in this church that Richard III was said to have prayed before the Battle of Bosworth in 1485 (it did not seem to do him much good!). If, however, you are eager to proceed, then turn sharp right just before Sutton Cheney along Ambion Lane, signposted 'Shenton'. After about ½km you will see Cheney Lane Bosworth Battlefield carpark on your left. Go into this and bear right and down to the bottom where there is a small gate and the start of a bridleway. Follow this on a good track along the edge of fields and through four gates to arrive at the Battlefield visitors centre (another tea stop?). Turn right and follow the drive downhill for about 100m. When you come to a large tree, go left and follow a grassy track uphill alongside a field boundary. When you reach a gate on your right, go through the gate. Although this bridleway is a right of way (and indeed is used by horses) it is also used by visitors to the battlefield, particularly at weekends. In fact, it might be a good idea to take time out to read the displays which give a graphic description of the Battle of Bosworth Field. In any event, take great care and GO SLOWLY! Follow the track round through several gates, down the hill, across a farm track

20

and to Shenton Station. This is the end of the recently extended Shackerstone steam railway, so take care when crossing the track or your bike might get damaged! Go through the carpark and onto the road.

Turn right at the road and continue down past the field on the left where King Richard fell (this is the bit where he cried 'A horse! A horse! My kingdom for a horse'). Climb uphill slightly to a junction where you go left for Shenton. Pass under the aqueduct and follow the road down to the T-junction. You have a choice here of going left to the Whitemoor Antique Centre for further quick refreshment (can you stand it?) or right if you want to continue on the route. Follow the road round left, then right for Sibson. After about 1km you come to Stubble Hill farm on your right and a bridleway. Follow this, forking right, and continue around the edge of the field on a good track. Go over a stream and past some stables to a single-file track through some oak trees. Eventually you reach a road (this last section can be a bit chopped up) where you turn right and continue up to bridge 37 on the Ashby canal.

Go down onto the towpath and turn left for Market Bosworth. Follow the path on a good track, but take care where it passes under the bridges as these are quite low and the paths become a little narrow. This track has recently been renovated and there are many places to stop and have a rest or picnic. There are also a few pubs situated not far from the canal. After approx. 6½km you reach bridge 52 at Shackerstone where you can stop for refreshments at the railway station and admire the trains and so forth or, if you prefer, visit the Rising Sun in the village. In any event, continue along the canal towpath until you reach the next bridge where you finally leave the canal.

Follow the road north over the railway bridge and for about 300m, until you see a drive signposted for Tivey's Farm. This is in fact an unclassified county road which eventually leads to Odstone. Go past the farm and under the railway bridge – this can be very messy in wet weather. Follow the obvious track and after a while it bears left and starts to climb towards Odstone Hall. The track goes right, around the grounds of the old hall to a bridle gate which leads onto a lane. Follow the lane into the hamlet of Odstone and a crossroads. Continue straight across for Ibstock but after about 1km you will see a track on your right. Follow this wooded, green lane (called Green Lane!) down to a ford and climb up on a stony track, eventually reaching a road junction. Cross straight over and return south along small lanes via Carlton to Market Bosworth and the start.

22

Ashby Canal at Far Coton

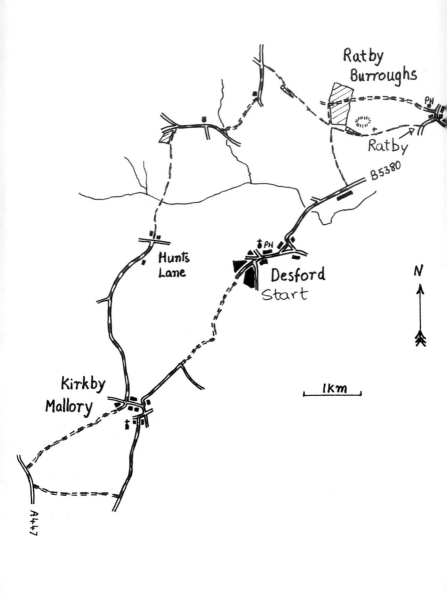

2. Leicester Forest

Route Summary
Desford, Ratby, Ratby Burroughs, Merry Lees, Kirkby Mallory, Stapleton, Desford.

Details
Grade – moderate, but can be difficult in wet.
Time – 3 hrs.
Distance – 28km.
         off road – 18km.
         on road – 10km.
Terrain – very gently undulating.
Surface – good unclassified roads, soft woodland bridleways.
Start Grid Reference – SK 479033.
Maps – Leicester & Coventry area L140.

Introduction
This route is situated on the very outskirts of Leicester. The land to the west of the city is generally flat, arable countryside with a little light industry, and it is perhaps surprising, therefore, that it is possible to produce such a pleasant and enjoyable route. In fact it is quite easy to escape the noise of modern day life and discover the quiet, old tracks that can be found in this area. The route uses a mixture of small country lanes, unclassified county roads and woodland bridleways. The latter can provide quite a challenge, in the wrong kind of conditions! The bridleways around Ratby are well used by horse riders and can be heavy going in the wet, and bone-jarring after a drought. The Ratby loop may seem a little contrived, but to leave it out would be to miss the pleasant ride to and from Ratby Burroughs, and the pub in the village!

25

Route Description

The route starts in the village of Desford, about 13km west of the centre of Leicester. From the new roundabout in the village go east and take the first left (straight on), the B5380 for Kirby Muxloe. Go down to a T-junction and left following the road down to Newtown Unthank. After ½km (opposite some factories – not a pretty bit this!) is a track on the left signposted 'Woodland Farm'. This partly tarmacked track is a bridleway and thankfully takes you away from civilisation and into the woods of Ratby Burroughs. The track goes past a house and eventually does a sharp right turn for Woodland Farm. Turn to the right and continue straight on where there is a blue waymarker, following the side of the field and towards the woods. After going through a small gate you descend and arrive at a bridleway junction.

Turn right here and follow along the edge of a field, with the boundary on your left, until you arrive at a large iron gate at the entrance to a wood. Continue straight on into the woods and then follow the edge of the wood, along a path which can be difficult in wet. After a short while the track leaves the wood via a small iron gate and enters a field. Follow along the bottom of the field by the side of a small stream. The track goes through several more bridle gates, all signposted with blue waymarkers, until you reach a more definite track. Eventually the track joins the road where you go left for the village of Ratby.

In the village go left, and then first left past the Bulls Head pub along the little lane called Burroughs Road. Stop at the Plough Inn if you are in need of refreshments and then continue along tarmacked road. The road fords a brook and then continues uphill to the woods of Ratby Burroughs again. The tarmac ends and becomes a firm track which has now been re-graded as a bridleway. When the track leaves the woods it continues to the ancient moated farm of Old Hays, reputed to have been a home of Lady Jane Grey. Do not continue along this track but turn left down the edge of the wood along a bridleway, to a small bridle gate and into the wood. The track brings you to a stream and almost in a full small circle (but a very worthwhile one). Go right and over the stream and along a wooded track, which can be extremely soft in places. The track goes through a golf course so keep your helmet on. After struggling through several soft bits for approx. 1½km, you arrive at a road.

Turn left at the road. After about ½km, just past a house, turn right and down a little wooded track. This delightful little unclassified road is called Coley Lane. At the bottom you pass Coley Cottage and here you have a

26

difficult choice – well actually not that difficult! The lane appears to ford a small river, but to the right is a footbridge. Ford the river if you feel like disappearing up to your armpits in mud or, more prudently, use the footbridge. The lane leads onto a road, where you go right for Merry Lees. Go over the railway bridge and up the hill to the top, where there is a junction. The main road bears right with a road straight ahead. You in fact turn left through a gate with a blue bridleway marker. The bridleway is not obvious, so head straight across the field to the far right-hand corner, go through a bridle gate and along the edge of the field to another gate and a farm track. Cross this, through a gate and across a short stretch of field to a double gate. After going through this and along the field boundary to a further gate, you go leftish down the side of a ploughed field to another gate and a large field. Head straight down the field to the bottom and a stream. Squelch your way through the stream and mud, or more sensibly, use the footbridge. Then carry on up the track, through a gate and along a lane to the main road.

At the road go across and down a lane signposted 'Brascote and Kirkby Mallory'. After about 3km you arrive at Kirkby Mallory village (famous for its racetrack which you cannot fail to hear on a Sunday afternoon) and a junction. Go straight across and down Stapleton Lane where it says 'Unsuitable for Motors'. The tarmacked road passes the racetrack (free views of the bike racing!) and just past the farm, becomes a good sand and gravel track. Follow this down the hill to a gate by a stream and some woods, a rather tranquil location. Go through a second gate and bear left on a vague track which takes you past a farm to the main road (A447). Go left on the road and after a few hundred metres turn left up a tarmacked lane (no signpost). Just after some houses the tarmac gives way to a good dirt track, but unfortunately this does not last long. Due to the somewhat inexpert use of off road vehicles the track can be quite rutted. After a tricky descent and about 1½km you reach the road at the bottom, where you go left and return to the south of the village of Kirkby Mallory. In the village go right, then left for Newbold Verdon, and then first right down Desford Lane. Follow the lane to a sharp right bend at Fairfields and continue straight on along a track signposted 'Unsuitable for Motors'. This excellent track goes over a little ford, eventually becomes tarmacked, and leads back to Desford and the start of the route.

Field road from Kirkby Mallory

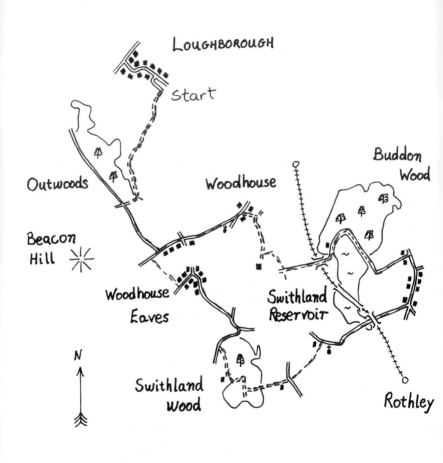

LOUGHBOROUGH

Start

Outwoods

Woodhouse

Buddon Wood

Beacon Hill

Woodhouse Eaves

Swithland Reservoir

N

Swithland Wood

Rothley

1 km

3. Charnwood Forest

Route Summary
Loughborough, Woodhouse Eaves, Woodhouse, Swithland Reservoir, Swithland, Swithland Wood, The Brand, Woodhouse Eaves, Loughborough.

Details
Grade – easy.
Time – 2½ hrs
Distance – 24km.
        off road – 13km.
        on road – 11km.
Terrain – small hills and woodland.
Surface – gravel tracks, open fields and woodland paths.
Start Grid Reference – SK 526176.
Maps – Nottingham & Loughborough area L129.

Introduction
The land to the north and west of Leicester rises gently to form a clump of hills called the Charnwood Forest. The highest landmark, Beacon Hill, may only be a little above 900ft, but they are generally regarded with affection by the people of Leicester and have been referred to as 'Little Matlock'. First inspection may give the impression that Charnwood could be an ideal location for off road biking – however, this is not quite the case. Although there are many footpaths in the area, bridleways do not abound. Until recently, mountain biking was allowed on specified tracks on Beacon Hill. Unfortunately, due to the inconsiderate behaviour of a few, bikes are now banned from this excellent area. It is, however, possible to combine small lanes and bridleways to form a route which provides fun and shows just a little of the beauty of the area.

Although the start of this route may not be very promising, situated as it is on the edge of a housing estate on the outskirts of Loughborough, it actually follows some surprisingly varied countryside. The route uses solid bridleway tracks and small roads and is therefore usually quite easy to ride, even after very wet weather. The route follows bridleways and roads below Beacon Hill to Woodhouse Eaves and Woodhouse and then continues off road to Swithland Reservoir. A short section on road takes us to Swithland and on good bridleways through the nature reserve of Swithland Wood, to return to the start via Woodhouse Eaves.

Route Description

Park at the carpark at the end of Moat Road, just off Valley Road. Follow the track running roughly south by the side of the recreation ground. The stony track, bordered by hedges, opens out and follows alongside a copse to a gate. Continue along, climbing gently below the Out Woods until the track divides. Go left and across the field on a good track towards some houses and the woods. After negotiating a couple of gates, go past the houses, bear right and up to a lane. Turn left here and follow Break Back Lane down to Woodhouse Eaves. Go left again at the main road and continue on down to Woodhouse.

Not long after the left-hand bend in Woodhouse is a lane on the right, Vicary Lane. Follow this track to a T-junction and go right for Rushey Field Manor. Just before the farm, go through a gate on the left and follow the bridleway for Swithland along the bottom of the field. Before the first field boundary, turn right and go up the field to a gate. Follow a grassy track to another gate and onto a lane. Go left here and follow the poorly surfaced lane, over the Great Central Railway and down to Swithland Reservoir.

Follow the lane north-east then turning right around the reservoir, admiring the attractive scenery, with Beacon Hill in the distance and, if you are lucky, a steam train crossing the viaduct. At the end of the reservoir take the sharp turn left uphill to the main road. Go right at the junction and down the road to Rothley Plain. At the junction go right for Swithland and Woodhouse Eaves and follow the road down to the south end of the reservoir. Stop here to feed the ducks if you want, and then continue on to Swithland. Just past St Leonards church is a bridleway on your left but, if you are in need of refreshments, the Griffin Inn is but a short distance up the road!

Go through the gate and along the bridleway between houses and then

Bridleway towards Out Woods

across a field, looking out for Swithland Hall on your left. Go through another small gate and then along a good, rocky track to a road. At the road go right, then almost immediately left along a bridleway past a house. This narrow but good track leads into Swithland Wood which is a nature reserve and a remnant of the ancient Charnwood Forest. The wood is a favourite with walkers, horse riders and bikers as well as wildlife. The many bridleways are clearly marked with yellow posts, so please keep to them and resist the temptation to go elsewhere. Follow the yellow posts uphill to a T-junction where you go right. After a short distance fork left, then almost immediately fork right and follow the track down and up to a small bridleway crossroads. Go right here, through a gate and along a good track by the side of a caravan park, eventually to a road.

At the road go right and down the hill past The Brand, a favourite spot with local rock climbers, to a junction. Here you go left and then left again for Woodhouse Eaves. Stop off at the Wheatsheaf Inn if you are in need of further refreshments and then continue up and down to the crossroads in Woodhouse Eaves. Turn left here and about 50m past the Curzon Arms is Mill Lane on your right. Go up this steep little hill, called Windmill Hill, which becomes a track and leads into the woods. Take a rest at the top on the bench (you may well need it if you have visited all the pubs en route!) and then leave the wood via a small gate. Go down the field to another two gates and a small carpark and onto the B591, where you go right. Take the next road left up Break Back Lane and return via the bridleway you started out on to Loughborough.

34

Entering Swithland Wood

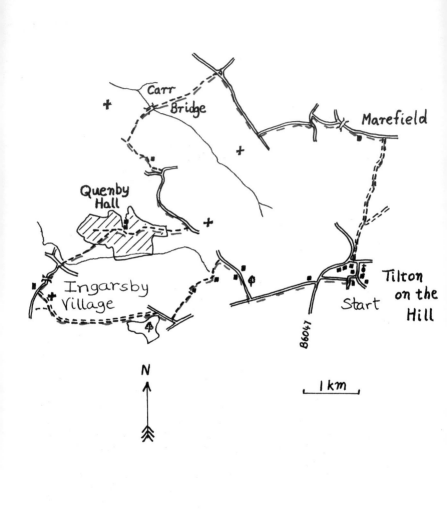

Carr
Bridge

Marefield

Quenby
Hall

Ingarsby
Village

Tilton
on the
Hill

Start

B6047

N

1 km

4. Tilton and Quenby

Route Summary
Tilton on the Hill, Sludge Hall Hill, Old Ingarsby, Quenby Park, Carr Bridge, Marefield, Tilton on the Hill.

Details
Grade – moderate.
Time – 3 hrs.
Distance – 24km.
        off road – 14km.
        on road – 10km.
Terrain – gently rolling hills.
Surface – bridleways across pasture and green lanes.
Start Grid Reference – SK 743057.
Maps – Kettering, Corby & surrounding area L141.

Introduction
The land to the east of Leicester is altogether much quieter and seemingly slightly less affected by ravages of modern day agriculture than that to the west. As one goes east, the land starts to rise gently and the houses on the outskirts of the city soon give way to fields and quiet, little lanes and villages. Here the fields are often small and there is much evidence of old, long deserted villages and tracks. In fact, there are so many tracks in the area it is difficult to decide which to use for the best possible route. This particular route starts at Tilton on the Hill, which has the reputation of being the highest village in the county, at about 700ft above sea level.

An alternative title for this route could have been 'An exploration of the deserted villages of Leicestershire', as there are many such in the area. A prime example is Ingarsby, which was originally settled by the Danes in the late

37

9th century and depopulated in 1469 when the Abbey of Leicester, who owned the manor, decided to enclose the area for sheep and cattle farming. The old hall still remains and there is clear evidence of the village in the neighbouring fields. Other deserted villages en route include Baggrave, Lowesby and Cold Newton, the latter particularly worth a visit.

Route Description

Start at the crossroads in the centre of Tilton on the Hill and go south, past the church and through the village. Take the first right and then, after going sharp left, take the next right, along Back Road to the B6047. Go left here, then right and along Tilton Lane. You will notice that after about 200m there is a gate on the right which leads into a field. This is in fact a gated road which leads past Hamner's Lodge Farm and on towards Cold Newton village. Although this village is almost too good to be missed and is well worth a visit at a later date, our route continues along the road to a crossroads, where we go right. Enjoy a speedy descent down Sludge Hall Hill, past the farm, and after about 300m you will see a track on the left. Go through the red double gates where there is a bridleway sign and along the firm track which then splits – left leading up towards Cold Newton Grange and right leading straight ahead. The bridleway, as shown on the map, goes left and through a gate on the right just before the farm. According to the map, the bridleway now crosses the arable field to the far right-hand corner, where there is a gate in the right-hand boundary. The occupants of the farm, however, have indicated that most users of the bridleway continue straight on at the division in the track and then along the bottom of the field to this gate. At any rate, go through the gate and follow the edge of the field with the boundary now on the left towards a farm. Go through two sets of large gates, along in front of the farm, and then bear left and up to a small red gate and a solid track. Go right and follow the track along to the road.

At the road go right and after about 300m you will see a gate on the left and a wide, grassy track across a field. Follow this ancient road to arrive at a gate and then continue straight on along a line of old trees. At the next gate continue along the top of the field on a grassy track, which still shows evidence of the original road, to another gate. Continue following a line of posts down to a gate where you go right and along a track between trees. After going through a couple of gates you cross the medieval village of Ingarsby, still clearly visible as a mass of bumps and hollows. The track leads to Ingarsby Old Hall and the road.

Carr Bridge "crossroads"

Go right on the road and follow it round, under a railway bridge and down to a T-junction. Just opposite is a bridleway sign. Follow the bridleway over a stream and uphill, through a couple of gates, climbing towards Quenby Hall. Eventually you arrive at a small red bridle gate which leads onto the main drive. Go right and along the drive towards the rather grand-looking hall. Bear right before the main gates and go through a small bridle gate and around the southern perimeter of the hall to regain the track at the back. Follow this track east through a couple of gates to arrive at a road. A left turn takes you along a road to a junction at White's Barn.

At the junction go right for Lowesby and just past the trees, on the left, is a bridleway sign. Follow this through the woods to a small gate, into a field and on to another gate. Cross the drive in front of Inkerman Lodge, through a small gate, and then bear right across the field. Go through another gate, bear left, cross a field then through another gate and across to a junction of bridleways. The bridleway ahead leads to Baggrave, another medieval village site but our route goes right. Follow down the left-hand edge of three fields. At the bottom of the last one you follow the track right and up to a gate. Go through this and bear slightly right to descend to a very old bridge, Carr Bridge, and, incongruously, a road signpost! Why this should be here is not clear, except that it marks the intersection of our bridleway and a footpath from Baggrave to Lowesby, and was obviously an important junction in the past. At any rate, we continue straight up the hill following the left-hand side of the field on a reasonable track through four gates, to arrive at a road.

Go right and along the B6047 for about 1km and then turn left for Marefield. Follow the pot-holed road down to a junction where you go left. Then turn right and along gated roads to the hamlet of Marefield. In Marefield follow the lane until, about 300m past the buildings, you see a bridleway sign on your right. Go through a gate and down a good stony track, fording a couple of streams. Continue on uphill (a nice little hill climb), eventually arriving back at the start of the route in Tilton on the Hill.

Bridleway from Marefield to Tilton on the Hill

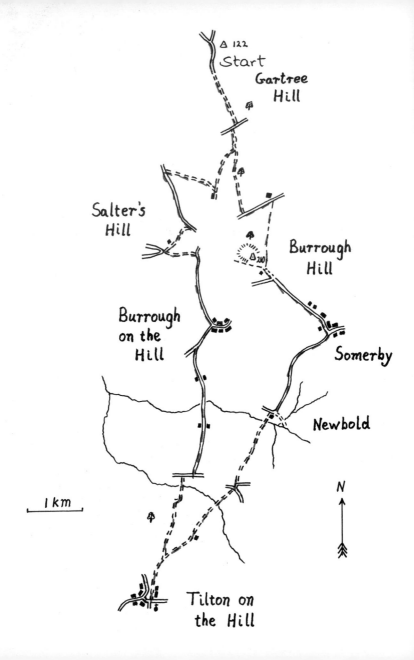

△ 122
Start
Gartree
Hill

Salter's
Hill

Burrough
Hill

△ 210

Burrough
on the
Hill

Somerby

Newbold

1 km

N

Tilton on
the Hill

5. Burrough Hill

Route Summary
Melton Mowbray, Gartree Hill, Burrough Hill, Somerby, Newbold, Tilton on the Hill, Burrough on the Hill, Salter's Hill, Gartree Hill, Melton Mowbray.

Details
Grade – difficult.
Time – 3½ hrs.
Distance – 27km.
        off road – 16km.
        on road – 11km.
Terrain – rolling hills, farm land and green lanes.
Surface – green lanes, grass and gravel, field bridleways.
Start Grid Reference – SK 755157, L129.
Maps – Nottingham & Loughborough area L129, Kettering, Corby & surrounding area L141.

Introduction
The route starts in Melton Mowbray and makes extensive use of the excellent unclassified county roads that extend southwards to Tilton on the Hill. Although there are many bridleways in the area, for example, between Owston and John O'Gaunt, these must be treated with care and are only for the truly committed mud-plodders! A highlight of the route is Burrough Hill. This is a site of archaeological interest and is managed by Leicestershire County Council. The top of the hill is an Iron Age fort and there is evidence of occupation from the 3rd century BC to the 4th century AD. More recently the area within the fort was used for country sports in the 16th and 17th centuries and also for the Melton Hunt Races. Nowadays, the whole area is protected by law so NO BIKES, except on the bridleways! The hill stands at a

43

magnificent height of 690ft above sea level and provides a grand view of the surrounding countryside. Take time to visit the viewpoint and have a picnic, but keep off your bike. Further south, the route makes good use of some excellent unclassified county roads which lead from Newbold to Tilton on the Hill via Red Lodge Road, and back via Marefield Lane.

Route Description

The route begins to the south of Melton Mowbray, just off the B6047, at grid reference SK 755157. At the end of the road a track goes left and continues roughly southwards (called Sandy Lane on the 1:25 000 map). The track passes through a few gates and along the left-hand side of some fields. It then climbs over Gartree Hill and eventually down a rutted lane to a road. Turn right and then first left down a green lane. This delightful track (at first!) passes through a couple of gates and down into a dip which can be boggy. Unfortunately, this lane can get difficult in the wet, as it is well used by horses. Struggle on and directly ahead you will see Burrough hill, an impressive little ridge in these parts.

After 1½km you arrive at a road where you have two possibilities. The first is to go left and towards Home Farm. Just past the farm and on the right is a bridleway which crosses an arable field, leading up towards Burrough Hill. In autumn and winter, when the field has probably been ploughed, this can be almost impossible and should only be attempted by the really determined! After a dry spell in summer, however, it is quite rideable. At the top of the field you enter the Dalby Hills Country Park via a small bridle gate. Continue straight on, across a path and up the hill, following the bridleway to arrive at a gate. This leads into an open field, the other side of which you cannot see at first, due to the shape of the hill. Have faith and carry straight on across and you will see a smaller gate. Continue on through this and down another field and up to a further gate. After going through this, aim for the main farm buildings straight ahead and the track which goes right for Burrough Hill or left to the carpark.

The second possibility would involve going right at the lane and towards Moscow Farm. Bear left at the farm and after 500m a road comes in from the right. Continue straight on and after another 500m or so there is a crossroads, although it does not immediately look like it at first. This is in fact a very ancient road called Salter's Road. The tracks are signposted 'Unsuitable for Motor Vehicles'. The track going right and up Salter's Hill says 'Field road to

44

Thorpe Satchville' (we will meet this on our return journey) and that left 'Field road to Burrough Hill'. Go left and along the left-hand side of the field, through a gate and up past the top of Burrough Hill to the track which leads to the carpark.

From the Burrough Hill carpark continue straight on along the road for Somerby. As you come into the village the road bears left (to the Stilton Cheese Inn!) but you turn right (a signpost advertises the Somerby Riding School) and along a tree-lined road which leads down to Newbold (change to map L141). At Newbold the road bears right and just after the house you will see a gravel road on the left. There is a signpost marked 'Unsuitable for Motor Vehicles' here but it was playing dead the last time I saw it! Follow the gravel track down over a muddy ford and on uphill on a good track to a road – go right here. Then at the junction where the road for Halstead continues straight on, take this but turn immediately right and through a metal gate. Follow the right-hand field boundary to the bottom, through a muddy ford and then a gate. Carry on uphill along a lane, through a gate, over an old railway bridge and up past Red Lodge Farm, from which the lane derives its name. The lane continues on tarmac and eventually arrives at Tilton on the Hill.

Stop for refreshments in the village if you like or take time to visit the 12th century church of St Peter, which apparently has some interesting gargoyles. Then return via the lane by which you entered the village. Where the lane divides, go left and down a gravel track, called Marefield Lane. This fords a couple of streams and arrives at the road near Marefield. Turn right and then take the first left along a lane for Burrough on the Hill. At Burrough Court turn right, then first left for Great Dalby, and zoom down the hill. At the Salter's Road junction at the bottom of the hill go left where it is signposted 'Field Road to Thorpe Satchville'. Climb the excellent track up Salter's Hill to the lane at the top, where you turn immediately right and go along a good track to a gate. Cross a field to another gate and through this to a green lane. The track becomes grassy and bears right after another gate and out onto a road, where you go left. After about 1km you will see a metal gate on the right. Go through this and follow the obvious track through three gates and downhill to some farm buildings. Here you go left and along a tree-lined green lane. The track goes through a gate, beyond which it can be very boggy, but eventually opens out and onto the track that we started out on. Turn left here and return via the track and Gartree Hill to Melton Mowbray and the start of the route.

Field road to Thorpe Satchville

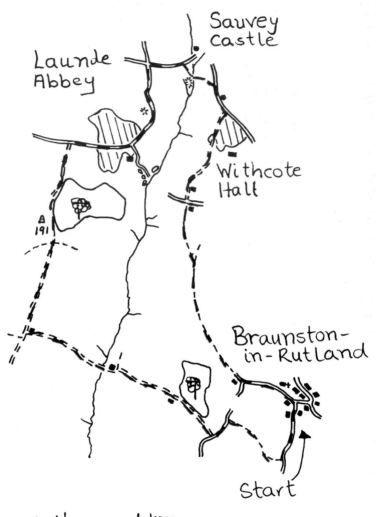

Sauvey Castle

Launde Abbey

Withcote Hall

Braunston-in-Rutland

Start

A 191

N

1 km

6. Launde Abbey

Route Summary
Braunston-in-Rutland, Withcote Hall, Sauvey Castle, Launde Park, Leigh
Lodge, Braunston-in-Rutland.

Details
Grade – moderate.
Time – 2 hrs.
Distance – 19km.
        off road – 14km.
        on road – 5km.
Terrain – gently rolling hills.
Surface – field edges and hard-pack tracks.
Start Grid Reference – SK 833066.
Maps – Kettering, Corby & surrounding area L141.

Introduction
The start of this pleasant little route is in Rutland, a county that has never
quite accepted being just another district of Leicestershire! The majority of
the off road is on field-edge bridleways, some of which can be a little difficult
in wet but on the whole are very good. The bridleway which runs along the top
of the hill towards Ridlington, for example, is mostly solid track and provides
fine views of the surrounding countryside. Other interesting sights to be seen
on the route include Launde Abbey, which nestles in a hollow of hills and is
surrounded by parkland and woods. The original priory was founded in 1119,
but was dissolved by Henry VIII in 1538. The house is 17th century and is
owned by the Diocese of Leicester. Also worth looking out for, although
slightly hidden by trees, is Sauvey Castle. Nothing remains of the castle itself,
but the motte and bailey construction, which uses the confluence of two
streams for a moat, can be clearly seen.

Route Description
Start at the Blue Ball Inn in Braunston-in-Rutland, a charming village with many pretty little cottages. Take the Leighfield and Ridlington road south out of the village and where the road goes left you continue straight on along a no through road. The road soon deteriorates and becomes a track and then a bridleway which follows a couple of long fields. This section is probably the most difficult part of the route when wet. At the end of the second field bear left through a gap and into a field with a much used track along the left-hand side. Follow this up to the top left corner, through a gap on the left and into a large ploughed field. Fortunately, the right-hand edge is fenced off and (hopefully) not ploughed. Continue along this with the boundary on the right, through a gap and straight on to the end of the field. Follow the boundary round left past a new gate to a second gate. Go through this and zoom downhill, with a field boundary on the left, to the bottom. Here you will find a gap on your left which leads through to the track from Withcote Lodge. Go right (straight on) and along the track to a house and a lane.

Opposite is a lane with a signpost saying 'Bridle Road to Withcote'. Follow this, past the farm with interestingly painted farming equipment in the front garden, to a gate. Continue along a tree-lined track until you arrive at some barns, with a view of the pool and Withcote Hall ahead (it can be a bit mucky here!). Turn left just past the barns and follow the edge of the pool round to a pair of large gates. Continue straight on along a stony track across parkland and in front of the house. You arrive at a paddock, go through two gates, and onto a drive. This takes you past a house and stables to arrive at the road.

Turn left at the road and go uphill and then down to the bottom, about ½km. At the bottom is a bridle gate on the left which leads into a field. The way ahead is not too clear at this point – you should cross diagonally right to a couple of gates. Go through the left-hand gate and follow the field boundary on your right to another gate, which takes you down into a little dell with a stream. Continue straight on through a gate and out into a field where the site of Sauvey Castle is just to your left. Bear right and follow along beside the stream to a small gate and then cross the field to another gate and the lane.

Go left at the lane and uphill, taking first left for Launde Abbey. Zoom down the hill and struggle your way up the other side, eventually arriving at Launde Abbey. Take time to admire the old building, set in front of parkland, with the monastic fish ponds on the left. Turn right in front of the abbey and sweat your way uphill. At the top of the hill turn left along a track with a

50

bridleway sign. Continue straight along this track, over a cattle grid and along by the side of Launde Park Wood. After a while the track bears to the left but you carry straight on, through a gate (no signpost) and across a field. Soon you arrive at a gate and cross a short stretch of field in front of the farm to another small gate. Continue along the bottom of the field by the side of the wood to yet another gate. Follow the bridleway to a gate in the corner. After passing through this you arrive at a bridle crossroads. Right leads down to Belton-in-Rutland and left down into the broad valley of the River Chater. We continue straight on along an excellent high level track (well anyway, it's high for the Midlands!).

Too soon we arrive at a large barn on the left, just past which is a track with a bridleway sign. It is very tempting to continue straight on, eventually arriving at Ridlington, but charming Rutland village though it is, it does not have a pub! Our route turns left through an impressive entrance and descends a hill to Leigh Lodge and the River Chater. At the bottom we cross over the river, go past the lodge and continue uphill along the drive. The track passes a farm and becomes tarmacked, eventually leading to the road. Go left at the road and down the hill. At the bottom of the hill is a bridleway sign on the right. Follow the track along the edge of the field to a gate. Continue along the tree-lined green lane, which becomes a long field, to another gate and then on to the road. Turn left and return to the start of the route in Braunston-in-Rutland, and a drink in the pub if it is still open!

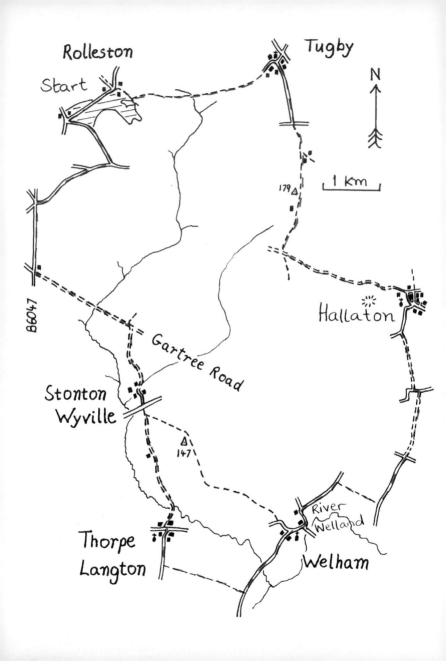

7. Rolleston

Route Summary
Rolleston, Tugby, Keythorpe Lodge Farm, Goadby Road, Hallaton, Hare Pie Bank, Slawston Hill, Welham, Thorpe Langton, Stonton Wyville, Gartree Road, Rolleston.

Details
Grade – difficult.
Time – 4 hrs.
Distance – 32km.
          off road – 19km.
          on road – 13km.
Terrain – gently rolling hills and farm land.
Surface – ranging from good solid tracks to field edges.
Start Grid Reference – SK 731004.
Maps – Kettering, Corby & surrounding area L141.

Introduction
South of the main A47 road running east of Leicester is an area containing many examples of fine, old unclassified county roads. Two used in this route, and worthy of note, are Goadby Road which runs from Goadby down into Hallaton, and the Gartree Road. The latter is in fact a Roman Road, now predominantly a minor road or bridleway, which stretches from Leicester, through Medbourne and eventually to Colchester. The section used in this route is little more than a good bridleway track. There are many variations on a theme here. The original route was to have included Noseley Hall and Park – however, the bridleway from Stonton Wyville to Noseley proved so difficult, due to ploughed fields, that it was decided to use the Roman Road.

55

Likewise, the bridleway which runs over the hill at Welham looked very tempting. Closer inspection, however, revealed that the bridleway cut across ploughed fields at the top and was therefore very difficult going. Other more hardy souls might like to try these possible alternatives!

A village worthy of note on this route is Hallaton which, together with the neighbouring village of Medbourne, is famous in these parts for the Hallaton Bottle Kicking contest. On the village green, near the conical butter cross, is a plaque which states the following:

'This ancient custom is a contest between the villages of Hallaton and Medbourne. Each Easter Monday after a service at the church the hare pie is presented to the rector to divide and distribute. A procession accompanied by a local band then collects the decorated bottles, small wooden barrels, and proceeds from the Fox Inn to the Hare Pie Hill where the pie is thrown to the crowds. This is the starting point of the contest which involves each team trying to get the bottle over the defined boundary. There are few rules and the result is based on the best of three such contests. The beer from the bottles is then drunk by the victors at the Butter Cross.'

This route actually uses a very old and quaint lane which runs from Hare Pie Bank down towards Medbourne.

Route Description

The route starts at the signpost at the crossroads in Rolleston. Follow the track signposted 'Bridle road to Tugby' which takes you past the beautiful old church of Rolleston and follows the perimeter wall of the hall. After going through a gate you proceed downhill to a signpost. Straight ahead is the bridleway to Goadby but we go left and through a gate with a signpost for Tugby. Follow the track down to a gate with a blue marker and continue along the edge of the wood, over a little stream and through another gate, again with a blue waymarker. So far, the track has been quite good, but unfortunately at this point it crosses two arable fields. Struggle as best you can (this is probably the most awkward part of the route) and soon you arrive at a stream. Go over a little footbridge, or if you are feeling a little more adventurous, ford the stream, and bear right following the grass track to a gate. Go through this and follow a good track straight on along the top of the fields, through two gates and then uphill towards the farm. Before you reach the farm you will see another bridleway on the right from Goadby, but we continue straight on. Just before the farm buildings, we bear right, through a gate and along a track which leads to a lane, and from there into the village of Tugby.

Go into the centre of the village, passing the Black Horse Inn and village stores, to a junction where we go right. Follow the road round, past another pub and out of the village. The road descends a gentle hill to a junction, where we go straight ahead on a good track signposted 'Field road to Keythorpe'. Continue straight on past Keythorpe Hall Farm and along a gravel track up the hill to eventually arrive at Keythorpe Lodge Farm. Go past the farm and straight ahead along a good track, passing through a couple of gates. Eventually you arrive at a junction of tracks, which is in fact the Goadby Road. Go left here and follow the track, which after a while becomes tarmacked, down the hill with good views ahead. The track crosses a ford and rises up to the village of Hallaton. Look out for Castle Hill, a superb example of a motte and bailey castle, on your right as you enter the village. It is thought that this was probably built in the 12th century to protect the surrounding iron workings. As you approach the village, go past some farm buildings and then turn right, down a poor road, which leads into the centre of Hallaton.

Hallaton is a very quaint and interesting little village and it is well worth visiting the village green, where you will see the Butter Cross and the plaque commemorating the Hallaton Bottle Kicking contest. After taking refreshments at the Bewicke Arms, take the road out of Hallaton towards Cranoe. As the road climbs out of the village and bears right, you continue straight on (left) and along a hedged track and down to a gate. (N.B. This lane is marked as a dead end on the 1:50 000 map but is continuous, as illustrated on the 1:25 000 map.) Follow the field boundary on your left through a couple more gates, along an ill-defined track, to arrive at a road. Go left and after 100m turn right and up a dirt lane. Follow this up past Slawston Hill to arrive at a crossroads. Continue straight across and down Green Lane. After about 1km you will see a bridleway crossing the road. Go right and through a gate, towards a derelict railway bridge. Follow the blue waymarker and continue on along the left-hand side of a couple of fields on a reasonable track (a bit chopped up by horses) to arrive at another road. Go left here and follow the road into the village of Welham, past the Old Red Lion pub.

At the junction carry straight on for The Langtons and Kibworth. As the road bears round to the right you will note a road leading straight on and this presents a choice. One option is to follow the Langton road round to the right and then take the bridleway across the top of the hill to Stonton Wyville. This provides a good hill climb and a fun descent, but unfortunately the section across the top is ill-defined and crosses arable (horrible!) fields. An easier alternative and one that provides a good view of the hills and more pleasant riding is as follows: Continue straight on where the road says 'Unsuitable for Motor Vehicles' and along Bowden Lane. After about 1km or so you will see a bridleway signpost on the right in some trees. Follow this hedged track, which soon opens out and continues along the left-hand edge of a large field on a reasonable track. After going through a couple more fields you arrive at a road. Go right here and up to Thorpe Langton.

At the village turn left and pass the Bakers Arms pub (if you can bear to!) and then first right down a lane signposted 'Unsuitable for Motors'. The track comes down to a ford, which you cross, and go left and through a gate. Follow the right-hand side of the field up to and along the top, soon to arrive at a gate on your right. Go through this and along the left-hand side of the field on a good track, past some barns, eventually arriving at the crossroads at Stonton Wyville. Cross over the road for the village.

In the village turn right where it is signposted 'Unsuitable for Motors', opposite the pretty little church. Follow the lane round past some barns and continue north on a good track, to eventually arrive at a rather unusual junction of tracks. Here you will find an old signpost which informs you that to your right is Glooston 1 mile, whilst to your left is Calton Curlieu (Manor House) 3 miles and Leicester 11¾ miles. This is the old Roman Gartree Road. Straight ahead is a bridleway which is supposed to lead to Noseley and which looks deceptively easy to start with, but is in fact of very dubious quality further on – not to be recommended except for the terminally masochistic! Our route goes left, following the rutted track through a couple of gates and down to a stream with a muddy ford and, fortunately, a footbridge. It is at this point that you perhaps begin to have a little sympathy for the drivers of the four-by-four vehicles that attempt this route – but perhaps not a lot of sympathy. Continue uphill on the obvious track through a couple more gates until you arrive at the B6047. Go right at the road and after a little over 1km, right again at Three Gates for Noseley. Take the second left along a gated road to Rolleston and finally right and down the tree-lined drive, to arrive back at the start, in the village.

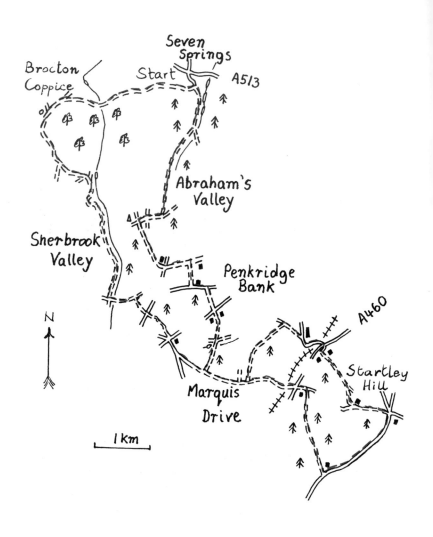

STAFFORDSHIRE

8. Cannock Chase

Route Summary
Seven Springs, Abraham's Valley, Penkridge Bank, Fair Oak Valley, Marquis Drive, Miflins Valley, Startley Hill, Marquis Drive, Sherbrook Valley, Mere Valley, Stepping Stones, Seven Springs.

Details
Grade – moderate.
Time – 2½ hrs.
Distance – 28km.
        off road – 26km.
        on road – 2km.
Terrain – hills and valleys.
Surface – good forestry tracks.
Start Grid Reference – SK 005205 L128.
Maps – Stafford, Telford & surrounding area L127, Derby & Burton upon Trent area L128.

Introduction
Cannock Chase is a justifiably popular area with walkers, horse riders and, more recently, mountain bikers. Situated so close to the towns of Rugeley, Stafford, Cannock and the conurbation to the north of Birmingham, it forms a convenient and easily accessible area of raised heathland and forest. It is not surprising, therefore, that it is so popular. The Chase covers about 26 square miles and is designated an Area of Outstanding Natural Beauty. The forest

and park contain a wealth of wildlife and there are several Sites of Special Scientific Interest. Unfortunately, conflicts between mountain bikers and other users of the area have arisen and the Forestry Commission, in consultation with all users, has had to limit access by mountain bikers to the main gravel tracks. This situation is under review and it is hoped that all bikers will act in a responsible manner, so as not to endanger access.

The Chase is well-known to local mountain bikers and, even with the current minor restrictions, there are so many tracks in this beautiful area that it is difficult to recommend the 'best route'. The route suggested takes in a large part of the Chase and uses legal bridleways almost exclusively. I would suggest that perhaps Sunday afternoon is not the best time to visit the Chase, but rather a quiet, warm summer's evening.

Route Description

The route starts at the Seven Springs carpark just off the A513 road to Stafford. Take the track which goes roughly south-east across the clearing to the woods in the left corner. Follow the track up Abraham's Valley by the side of the stream and past the pools. The track climbs steadily. Follow it ignoring any tracks to the left or right until you arrive at a T-junction where you go right. After a short climb, continue straight on at the crossroads and into the woods, very soon to arrive at trig point 199m. Go left here and along a wide gravel track which eventually bears left by the cadet huts and arrives at a crossroads. Continue straight on, going approximately east along Kingsley Wood Road, a gravel track. Take the right just before a smallholding, which leads you to the road, Penkridge Bank.

Go left and then after about 300m dive off down a track on the right. Follow this up over a little rise, then down again to another road with a track opposite. Go straight across the road, follow the track uphill to Fairoak Lodge and carry straight on between a house and some buildings. Very soon the track bears right, but the bridleway continues straight on downhill. Go down the track to arrive at Fairoak Pools and a junction of tracks. Continue straight on past the pool and climb uphill to arrive at a T-junction on Marquis Drive. Turn left here and after about 800m, take the second left down a broad track. Follow the downhill for 1½ km to arrive at a junction. Go right here and follow the track downhill until you come out at a road opposite some houses. A right turn here will bring you to the main A460.

Fortunately, we do not have to use the main road, but cross over to a slip

MOUNTAIN BIKES
ALL RIDERS MUST KEEP
TO BRIDLEWAYS AND
GIVE WAY TO WALKERS

road which takes you down to the start of the track at the bottom of the Miflins Valley. Go left here and up the valley, soon escaping the hassle of the road. Eventually you join up with Marquis Drive again, and continue to climb, soon arriving at a road junction. Go right and follow the road for about 1½ km, passing the drive to the Beaudesert Golf Club. Shortly after this you will see a track on the right which doubles back. Follow this for a short distance until you see a notice that warns you of low flying golf balls from the left (especially if you are on a mountain bike?). Keep your helmet on, your head down and scurry across the short stretch of fairway, keeping to the bridleway! Continue straight on into the woods and follow the obvious and superb descent all the way back down to the bottom of Marquis Drive, and then left to the main road.

Cross the road and go over the level crossing (take care!) and continue climbing up Marquis Drive. After a while the track begins to level out and eventually becomes tarmacked. Continue straight on until you reach the main road where you go right (straight on) (change to map L127). Very soon you come to a crossroads. Diagonally right is a track, signposted 'Heart of England Way', which leads into the woods. Follow this and at a junction do a dogleg right and then left, and continue on the bridleway. Soon you reach another junction, where you do a repeat performance. After a short distance you arrive at a road where you cross over and continue on downhill on the Heart of England Way. You arrive at a T-junction, where the route goes left and down to the Sherbrook Valley. Cross over a very small stream and go right and down a good track on the west side of the valley.

Follow this excellent track north and just after the track does a U-bend (an erosion control measure) you will see a small weir on your right. Just by this is a junction of tracks and you go ahead left and uphill to the top, where you join the Heart of England Way again. Go right here and cross over a small carpark. There now follows a long and sweeping descent with fine views down to a pool in the woods in the Mere Valley. Turn right for the Punch Bowl and where the track divides, go right again, along the Staffordshire Way. At the Stepping Stones, turn left, cross the ford and follow the track, which eventually takes you back to the Seven Springs carpark and the start of the route.

The Staffs Way

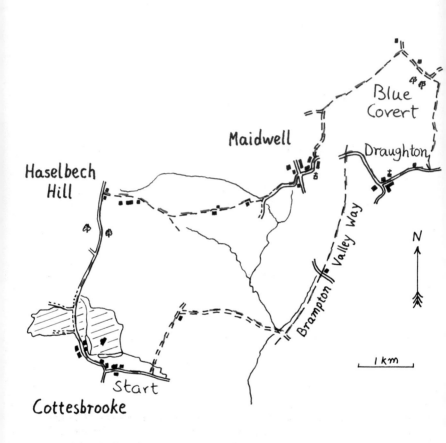

Blue Covert

Maidwell

Draughton

Haselbech Hill

Brampton Valley Way

N

1 km

Start

Cottesbrooke

NORTHAMPTONSHIRE

9. Cottesbrooke

Route Summary
Cottesbrooke Park, Brampton Valley Way (Hanging Houghton), Lamport Crossing, Draughton carpark, Draughton, Blue Covert, Maidwell, Haselbech Hill, Cottesbrooke Park.

Details
Grade – easy.
Time – 2½ hrs.
Distance – 25km.
        off road – 17km.
        on road – 8km.
Terrain – very gently undulating.
Surface – good gravel tracks, some grassy bridleways.
Start Grid Reference – SP 720733.
Maps – Kettering, Corby & surrounding area L141.

Introduction
This pleasant route is situated in historically interesting countryside to the north of Northampton, not far from the battlefield site of Naseby. The site marks the important confrontation between the Royalist and Roundhead forces during the Civil War in 1645 and, although not actually included in the route, the museum and monument are well worth a visit. Although the land is predominantly flat in these parts, there are small hills and ridges that provide good views of the surrounding countryside.

The route uses old unclassified county roads and bridleways to the east of Naseby, and sections of the Brampton Valley Way. The latter is a disused railway line that was purchased by the County Council in 1987 and developed as a route for walkers, cyclists and horse riders. Many cyclists use this easy linear track, but perhaps few have ventured to explore the possibilities beyond. Two country houses in the area that are worthy of note are Lamport House and Cottesbrooke. The route is based around the latter and, although the house is not open to the public, there are fine views of it and the surrounding park on the return journey.

Route Description

Leave the charming village of Cottesbrooke and follow the Brixworth gated road east. After about 1km you will see, on your left, some barns and a track with a signpost saying 'Unsuitable for Motors' and a byway signpost. Follow this past the barns on a partly tarmacked track, through a couple of gates and into a wood. Just past a derelict house the track forks and we go right. Follow the long and well-defined track down and across fields, eventually arriving at a little bridge. Just past this is the disused railway line, now the Brampton Valley Way. Go left and along this, shortly arriving at Lamport Crossing. Cross over the main road (take care!) and continue straight on, arriving at Draughton carpark after about 2km.

At the lane go right and uphill, soon to arrive at the village of Draughton. Bear left into the village and continue straight on past the church. About 1km outside the village you will see a track on the left-hand side, with metal posts, and a signpost saying 'Bridleway to Harrington'. Follow this concrete track past some derelict buildings and along an old World War II airstrip. Near the end of the runway there is a copse on the left, through which passes a narrow path which very soon leads to a solid track. Go left along this and by the side of Blue Covert. The track leads up to the new A1-M1 link road works, just before which you go left down an obvious track, along the right-hand side of a field. The track enters another field and becomes less defined, but soon enters some trees and arrives at the Brampton Valley Way again. Cross over this and continue straight on along a rutted but rideable track. At the far end of the large field the track divides and you go left, down the right-hand side of the field. Soon you reach a gate, through which the track continues across grazing land and arrives at another gate and a lane on the outskirts of Maidwell.

Go right and follow the road through the village to the main road. Note the

Bridleway near Maidwell. Repair time

interesting gate, by the side of which is a stone informing us that the gateway was restored by a Reginald B Lode and was opened in 1914 by Field Marshall Lord Grenfell. At the main road do a dogleg right and then left and follow the lane round left for Dale Farm. This takes you down through some trees, Dale Farm Conservation Area, to a junction and continues straight on uphill for the farm. The drive bears round to the right of the house and continues on up the slight hill. At the farm follow the direction of the bridleway signposts and bear to the right of the buildings. Just before the last barn follow the bridleway signposts which lead you along a track to the top of a field. Continue along the left-hand side of a couple of fields, with pleasant views on your left.

This next section is probably the most difficult part of the route. Basically, it involves continuing straight on along the side of arable fields but, fortunately on a reasonable track. At the end of the second field go through a gap on your left, and continue straight on along a narrower track on the right-hand side of the next field. The increasingly ill-defined track continues along the left-hand edge of another field, eventually arriving at a gap on the left and a bridleway signpost. Continue on for Haselbech along and around the right-hand side of this field, at the end of which you go right towards a solid track. Go left and towards a little white house and some woods – look out for Haselbech Hall in the distance on the right. Follow the drive, until it meets a lane, where you go left. This delightful gated road provides a fast descent back down into Cottesbrooke.

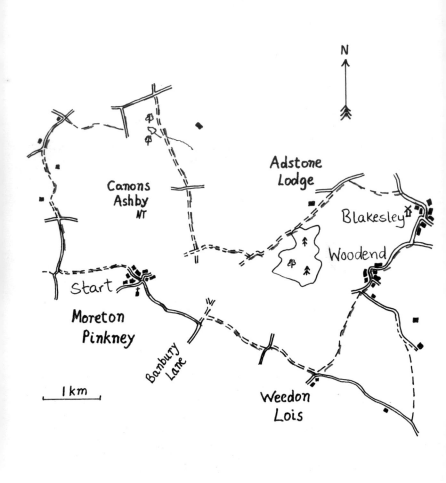

10. Canons Ashby

Route Summary
Moreton Pinkney, Crockwell Farm, Woodfordhill, Ashby Gorse, Canons Ashby, Adstone Lodge, Woodend, Weedon Lois, Moreton Pinkney.

Details
Grade – moderate (in good conditions).
Time – 2½ hrs.
Distance – 22km.
        off road – 16km.
        on road – 6km.
Terrain – very gently rolling countryside.
Surface – mostly byways, varying from good to very rutted and soft in wet.
Start Grid Reference – SP 575492.
Maps – Northampton & Milton Keynes area L152.

Introduction
This route is perhaps best appreciated on a warm sunny day in early summer, after a period of dry weather. During winter the landscape can be a little bleak and the going extremely soft, to say the least! Although centred around Canons Ashby, the route itself does not visit the pretty hamlet, but a quick detour to see the National Trust house is well worth the effort (if you are in a presentable state!). The name of the village derives from the priory of Augustinian canons that was established here in the 12th century, and the medieval church still remains. Canons Ashby is the home of the Dryden family, the most famous member of which was John Dryden, who was the Poet Laureate between 1670-1688. Being a National Trust property the house also has an excellent little tea shop!

    The route is based on the many byways that can be found in the area. Most of these are in excellent condition, butunfortunately, those to the south-east of Canons Ashby can be rather churned up, due to the over-enthusiastic use of four-wheel drive vehicles.

Route Description
Start in the village of Moreton Pinkney by The Olde House at Home public house (what better place to start!). If the pub is open, enjoy a quick refreshment, but if not perhaps this will provide the incentive to complete the route in reasonable time. Follow the main road south-west from the pub until you see Brook Street on your right. Follow this down to a ford, over the brook, and continue on a good, solid track until you reach a gate at a field. Go through the gate and carry straight on along a good track with the boundary on your right to a second gate and then down towards some trees. Here you bear right and up to the road by a disused railway bridge. Continue north down the small road and eventually up to a junction. Cross over and continue along the track towards Crockwell Farm.

Just before the farm, bear right and go up the steep little hill on a good track. At the top, continue on past Tile Barn and a small pool, eventually arriving at a road. Carry straight on for Preston Capes until you reach a road junction, where you go right and through a gate signposted as a byway. Follow the sand and gravel track to the bottom of the field where it divides. Right is a footpath, so we go left and up the hill. At the top continue straight on, on a less definite green track, past a house and onto the road, where you go left.

Follow the road a short distance to a T-junction and turn right. After about ½km there is another junction where you go right, through a gate signposted as a byway and follow the right-hand side of the field on an obvious green track. The track goes past Ashby Gorse with its pool, enters the wood and crosses a concrete drive. Continue straight on, along a good track down the right-hand side of a large field, eventually arriving at a road about ½km east of Canons Ashby. This last bit can be very soft. If time allows take a break and have a look around the old house and grounds – even stop for a cream tea! Otherwise, cross straight over the road and continue south on the track, again signposted as a byway (cars not allowed except for loading?).

The track is bordered by hedges and is deeply rutted in places, presumably by the over-enthusiastic use of four-wheel drive vehicles. After a while the track opens out into a field and follows down the right-hand side. At the bottom go through a gap, cross over the old railway line and continue up the

The byway past Crockwell Farm

right-hand side of another arable field. The track improves and at the end of the field you go through a bridle gate and onto an excellent unclassified road.

Turn left and follow the road, which is basically a stony track over a stream and eventually across a field to some trees. Here you arrive at a clearing which is really an old junction of byways. Turn left and follow a broad, hedged track (badly rutted in places), bearing right then left and then continue down the side of a field. Evidence that this is an ancient road is apparent from the old trees that line either side of the byway. Continue down past woods and between the remains of the old railway line and bridge and on up past a wood. In spring and early summer this wood is a mass of wild flowers and the track itself is adorned with clumps of cowslips. Do not pick the flowers, leave them for others to enjoy!

Continue on through a gate and past Adstone Lodge to arrive at a road. Go straight on (right) and after a few 100m you will see a bridleway on the right. Go through the gate and along the right-hand side of a field to arrive eventually at another gate. Go through this, across a short stretch of grazing land to a gate by a road and turn right. Follow the road into Blakesley (look out for the old windmill) and go right at the village green, for Woodend. Stop for more refreshments at the Bartholomew Arms, then bear right outside the village, soon to arrive at the village of Woodend.

Go right in the village and follow the road round for Weston. At the top of a rise and opposite some houses there is a lane on the left. Almost straight ahead, at the start of the lane, you will see some green gates on the right (no signpost). Go through these and along the right-hand side of the field on a good track to an old barn. Go through a gap and along the right-hand edge of another field to a bridle gate. This next section can be very difficult and it may be necessary to get off and push/carry at this point. Continue straight on, through the gate, by the side of a large arable field and then head straight across and down to the bottom. Here you will see a barbed wire fence with a primitive stile. The worst of this section is now over. Climb over the stile and cross the pasture to a ford with a bridge. Cross the stream and go left around the bottom of a field on a definite track. As you climb up the slight hill the track improves, until you reach a gate by a road junction near Weedon Lois.

Go right at the junction and along the tree-lined green lane to Moreton Pinkney. The definite track leaves the trees and continues along the right-hand edge of two fields, to arrive at a gate at a road. Cross over the road and go through a gate following the byway sign. Continue along the right-hand edge

Canons Ashby

of three fields passing through gates on a less than definite track but on grazing land. Eventually you arrive at a gate by some woods, through which you will find a very rocky path. If you close your eyes you could almost imagine you are on a technical bit on the Lakes – except that it is flat! Continue on the track to a clearing, which is a byway crossroads. Go left to the road, then right and soon you find yourself back in Moreton Pinkney, in time perhaps for a quick pint!

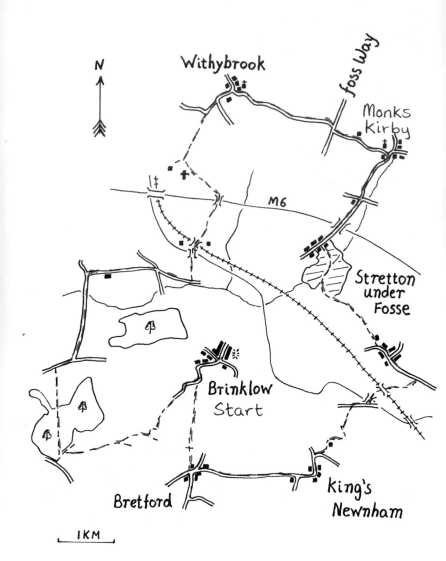

N

Withybrook

foss Way

Monks
kirby

M6

Stretton
under
Fosse

Brinklow
Start

Bretford

King's
Newnham

1KM

WARWICKSHIRE

11. Brinklow

Route Summary
Brinklow, Bretford, King's Newnham, Easenhall, Newbold Revel, Stretton under Fosse, Monks Kirby, Withybrook, Upper Smite Village, Coombe Abbey, Brinklow Heath.

Details
Grade – difficult.
Time – 3 hrs, depends very much on the state of the bridleways!
Distance – 30km.
        off road – 16km.
        on road – 14km.
Terrain – farm land.
Surface – bridleways along edge of fields and in woods.
Start Grid Reference – SP 435792.
Maps – Leicester & Coventry area L140.

Introduction
This route uses a cluster of bridleways around the village of Brinklow, just 10km east of Coventry. Horse riding is popular in this area so the tracks are reasonably well-defined. Unfortunately, as the land is low lying, in wet weather the tracks can also become extremely chopped up by the horses. This is especially true of the bridleway from Brinklow to Bretford, where there can be some quite impressively muddy puddles. After a period of dry weather, however, the tracks tend to be firmer and less bumpy, with only the occasional splash!

The bridleway from Easenhall to Stretton under Fosse requires a special mention. According to the definitive map, the right of way starts at Farm Lane, goes through the yard of Welkin Farm and over Tumley Hill. The owners of the land, Mr Postlethwaite & Sons at Welkin Farm, have indicated however, that they feel it would be easier for the public to divert slightly by using a path around the edge of the village cricket pitch, which they own, joining the excellent track which leads towards Stretton, and which is eventually joined by the bridleway proper. Signs have been erected to encourage this and the route is well-used by the locals. In fact, this private track is much better than the bridleway, but if in any doubt, follow the right of way.

Route Description

The route starts at the main junction in Brinklow. Go right on the Coventry road and almost immediately go left down Heath Lane. Follow the lane as it bears round to the left. Where the road turns sharp right, continue straight on along an unsignposted bridleway between hedges. The track, which is narrow and can be extremely soft in places, rises uphill gently and crosses another bridleway. Continue straight on and down, sharing the track with a muddy stream, to come out eventually by a house and at the main road in the village of Bretford. Go left and past The Queens Head pub. Where the main road, which is the Foss Way, turns left you continue straight on for King's Newnham. After about 2km you pass the remains of the old church at Newnham Hall and then the village. The road does a sharp left and rises uphill to a junction, where you go right. As the road bears further right, you continue straight on and along a track signposted by a bridleway marker.

Follow the bridleway down to some farm buildings, then turn sharp right past the last building (do not be tempted to continue straight on). The track proper is not obvious at first, but is quite passable and eventually, after following around the edges of fields used for grazing, arrives at a lane. Go right and after about 100m you will see a marked bridleway on the left. Follow this over the Oxford Canal, under the railway line and, where the track forks, go right and along a wooded track. Soon you arrive at a lane which takes you to the road.

Go left at the road and after less than a kilometre, you arrive at the attractive village of Easenhall. Go past the pub to the village green, bearing right where it is signposted 'Bridle Road to Stretton under Fosse'. The right of way goes through the yard of Welkin Farm and continues over the hill (see

introduction). However, most locals go left through a gate, and around the right-hand edge of the village cricket pitch, eventually arriving at a gate and left onto a superb hardpack track. This crosses open parkland to some woods and is joined by the bridleway proper. The track continues around the edge of Newbold Revel College and, where it enters the grounds at a gate, you bear left following the bridleway marker. Follow the track across the main drive of the College and continue through a gate and around the edge of the grounds. Soon you come to another drive, where you go left and up to the main road in Stretton under Fosse, by The Union Jack Inn.

At the main road, turn right and pass over the M6. Soon the road bears sharp right at a junction, but you continue straight on along a minor road, signposted Monks Kirby. When you arrive in the village of Monks Kirby, take the first left by the Denbigh Arms, for Withybrook. Soon you arrive at the Foss Way where you do a dogleg by going right, then left, and continue west along the lane to the quaint little village of Withybrook. After perhaps stopping at the pub for refreshments (excellent food!), go south-west along the B4112 for a short distance. As the road turns left, continue straight on along a lane. Soon this bears sharp right, but you continue straight on, through a double gate and along a bridleway. The track crosses a field, goes through another bridle gate and now, enclosed by trees, becomes firmer as you climb the hill. At the top you pass through a gate and into a field.

After about 50m there is another large gate with a bridleway sign on the left. Follow this grass track along the back of a wood, through two more large gates, and into a field. The bridleway skirts round the right-hand side of the field, through another large gate and again right and around the edge of the field. Eventually you reach a gap in the far corner of the field, which takes you over a bridge with excellent views of the M6 motorway (you don't get this kind of thing in the Lakes!). The track then continues down the left-hand side of a field, through a gate on the left, and towards some farm buildings to another gate. After going through this the track descends slightly, past the farm, and out onto a tarmacked track. Go right, over the railway line, and the Oxford Canal again, then follow the road down to a T-junction.

At the road go right and along to a crossroads where you go straight across for Coombefields. The road takes you past Peter Hall Farm to a junction with a lovely view of the Rolls Royce factory opposite (well, this is the heart of industrial Midlands, what else do you expect?). This may not be the most stunning section of the route, but it is well worth the effort for what is to

The track to Stretton under Fosse

follow! Go left and soon you reach another junction where you turn right for Coventry. After a few hundred metres and opposite the main entrance to Coombe Countryside Park, you will see an excellent sandy track on your left. This is called Twelve O'clock Ride on the 1:25 000 map, presumably because it runs almost north-south. Zoom along the track until you reach a gate at the entrance to a wood. Go through the gate and enjoy the ride through the woods, eventually arriving at a lane, where you go left. Near the end of the lane and just before a house, turn right and follow the track which goes around the side of the house. Things can get rather soft in places here, so be prepared to get slightly muddied! After a while you will see a bridleway on the right which leads down to Brandon – not long after this, there is a fork. Right and straight ahead leads to Bretford, but we bear left along a firm, but narrow tree-lined track. Soon you fork left again, then bear right, and follow the solid track along the edge of a field to a gate. The track becomes tarmacked and eventually leads back into Brinklow and the start of the route.

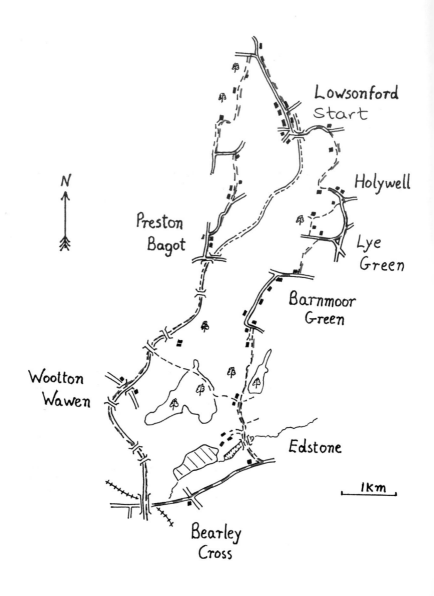

N

Lowsonford
Start

Holywell

Lye
Green

Preston
Bagot

Barnmoor
Green

Wootton
Wawen

Edstone

1 Km

Bearley
Cross

12. Henley-in-Arden

Route Summary
Lowsonford, Bushwood, Preston Fields, Preston Bagot, Stratford Canal, Bearley Cross, Edstone, Barnmoor Green, Lye Green, Holywell, Lowsonford.

Details
Grade – easy.
Time – 2½ hrs.
Distance – 25km.
　　　　　　off road – 14km.
　　　　　　on road – 11km.
Terrain – gentle hills and canal towpaths.
Surface – good towpaths, gravel tracks, but soft woodland bridleways.
Start Grid Reference – SP 188678.
Maps – Stratford-upon-Avon & surrounding area L151.

Introduction
This attractive route makes extensive use of the charming Stratford-upon-Avon canal and is situated in the heart of the ancient Forest of Arden. Little of the original forest remains, but the area is wooded and the terrain gently undulating. A combination of bridleways, unclassified roads and canal towpaths makes for a relaxing ride with several pubs on the way, ideal for a summer's evening. The Stratford-upon-Avon canal was at one time owned by the National Trust, but is now administered by British Waterways, and can be used by bikers **upon the purchase of a permit**. Most of the off road is generally good, even after less than dry conditions; however, the bridleway from Barnmoor Green to Yarningale can cause problems. This is well-used by horses and, enclosed as it is by trees, can be extremely boggy. Discretion may be the better part of valour and a detour via Claverdon and Lye Green might be preferable.

Route Description

Start at Lowsonford by the rather interesting lock keeper's cottage on the Stratford-upon-Avon canal. Go north-west out of the village along the lane for Lapworth, and after about 1km turn left for Henley and along Bushwood Lane. After a little over 100m you will see the entrance to Bushwood Farm on the left, which is a bridleway. Follow the gravel track up past a house and a wood to the farm. A fenced-off track goes in front of the farmhouse and leads you onto an excellent track. Enjoy a rattling good descent on a gravel track which takes you to a small bridle gate. Follow the bridleway round right and past Coppice Corner Farm to the drive. Turn left on the drive, go over the disused railway bridge and down to the road.

Turn left and after a short distance, where the road bears left by some houses, you go right and down a gravel track. Cross a superb little ford (use the bridge if you must!) and continue on up a gravel track, which eventually brings you out at the end of a lane. Follow this lane down past some highly desirable residences to a junction, where you go straight on (right). The road descends a hill, past the Norman church at Preston Bagot and brings you to another junction, where you go left. Shortly, you arrive at the main A4189 road to Warwick, where you go left. After 100m you will see the impressive Manor House. The manor house and farm were built in 1550 by the order of the Earl of Warwick and was later the home of Ingram Bagot. Of more importance perhaps, is the fact that at the end of the lane by the side of the manor house and adjacent to the Stratford canal is the Haven Tea Rooms. Although the author has not had the pleasure of experiencing this establishment, the refreshments on offer seem ideal for the sport of mountain biking! To continue the route, we cross the main road opposite the manor house, go through a gate and descend the track to the towpath by the canal.

Follow the canal south, soon leaving the noise of the road far behind. This beautiful canal meanders its way through pasture land and woods and is quite charming on a sunny summer's evening. Take care, however, as the path can get narrow in places and unexpected obstacles could lead to a surprise dip in the murky waters. For those who tire easily there is a shortcut at canal bridge 51, where you can go left over the bridge, along a sometimes muddy track between trees, through a wood and down to Cutler's Farm. Those happy to continue follow the canal towpath to the bridge by the Navigation Inn, which is a favourite watering hole for those navigating the canals. Continue via the aqueduct over the main Stratford road. Shortly the towpath crosses to the left-

The ford on Preston Fields Lane

hand side (note the curious old road sign in the field on the right) and eventually arrives at the famous Bearley Cross aqueduct. This crosses a railway line and then a road. Descend the steps to the road and go right (east).

At the junction of the main road, continue straight on along the lane for Norton Lindsey. After about 1km, just past a farm, you will see a lane on the left with a bridleway signpost. Follow the drive down to a copse and by some tranquil lakes at Edstone then bear right for Cutler's Farm. This section can hardly be described as off road, but is extremely pretty and quiet. At the farm you will see the track on the left from the Stratford canal. Go past the farm, bearing right and onto a gravel track which climbs up the valley slightly to a couple of gates. Take the right-hand gate and go along the left-hand side of the field on a good track to another gate. Continue on a less distinct track across a pasture, through another gate and down a track to Chestnut Rise Farm. Bear right and down the lane to the road at Kington Grange, where you go left.

Follow the road round and eventually you arrive at the main road, where you go right. Fortunately, we do not stay on the road for long but, just past some houses on the left, there is a lane with a bridleway signpost. This next section can pose some real problems! The wooded track, although a bridleway, tends to consider itself more a swamp than anything else, even after dry weather. After some considerable struggling through bogs, the track improves and arrives at a lane. A possible alternative, for those wishing to avoid this section, is to remain on the road from Kington Grange into Claverdon, where you turn left for Lye Green. If you bravely struggled over the bridleway section, turn right when you arrive at the road and cycle the short distance into Lye Green. At Lye Green, you fork left in the village and travel north towards Holywell. At the crossing in Holywell you take the left fork heading north-west on a dead-end road past some buildings. This dead-end road eventually becomes a bridleway, which leads to a farm. Continue past the farm and bear right along a hedged bridleway, which descends to a small gate. Go through this and a further gate, to enter a field. Cross diagonally left to a gate and up the right-hand side of the next field. After going through another gate follow the drive down to the road, where you go left and back to the start of the route in Lowsonford.

Top: Lowsonford Lock
Bottom: Edstone

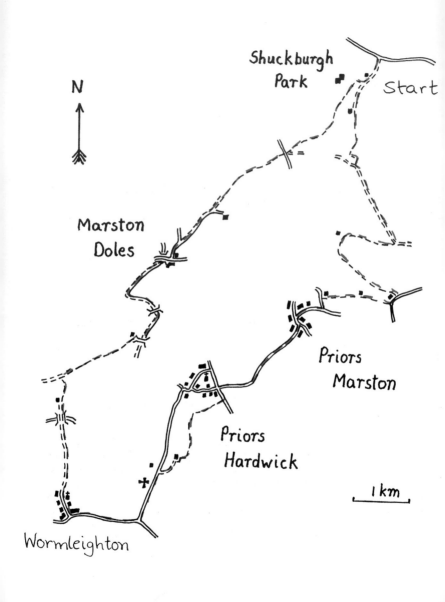

N

Shuckburgh Park

Start

Marston Doles

Priors Marston

Priors Hardwick

Wormleighton

1 km

13. Priors Marston

Route Summary
Shuckburgh, Marston Doles, Oxford Canal, Wormleighton, Stoneton, Priors Hardwick, Priors Marston, Shuckburgh.

Details
Grade – difficult.
Time – 3½ hrs.
Distance – 30km.
        off road – 22km.
        on road 8km.
Terrain – flat with a few bumps.
Surface – bridleways and tracks across mixed farm land, canal towpath.
Start Grid Reference – SP 503620.
Maps – Stratford-upon-Avon & surrounding area L151.

Introduction
This route is specifically designed for those who do not like hills and who have a particular liking for field bridleways! As can be seen, quite a significant part of the route is off road, with some excellent tracks, for example, towards Wormleighton and also from Hellidon. It must be said, however, that bridleways alongside and across fields are extensively used. In winter, or typical wet summer conditions for that matter, these tracks can get quite difficult. The fields in this area are a mixture of grazing and arable, but in most cases definite tracks are preserved, even where they cross fields. Exceptions to this can be found on the bridleway before it joins the excellent track into Wormleighton. However, these are quite short sections and it is well worth the battle, if only to enjoy the track which follows. The route visits several interesting and unspoilt villages – Wormleighton is of particular note. This

quiet little village has a rather curious tower, which is in fact a gate house to the old manor. Built by John Spencer in the 1500s, an ancestor of Lady Diana Spencer, most of the manor was destroyed at the time of the Civil War, and little more than the tower remains. The parish registers also record connections with another famous person, of George Washington's family.

Priors Hardwick and Priors Marston also deserve a special mention. Both of these fine villages contain many quaint little ironstone cottages, with some good pubs, and are well worth a quick detour.

Route Description

The route starts on the main A425 at a little lane just to the east of Shuckburgh Park. If car parking here is not possible, then an alternative start would be in Lower Shuckburgh itself, but this would involve riding on a little over a kilometre of main road. Starting at grid reference 503620, take the small lane south until you pass a cottage and track on the right, and continue on down to a gate. Go through this and then immediately right and through another gate, which is marked with a bridleway signpost. Follow an ill-defined track around the right-hand side of the pasture, through a gate and continue on up the field. At the top go through another gate and along the left-hand side of the field on a more defined track. Carry on through another field, now along the right-hand side, contouring around the hill until you arrive at a gate and out onto a road.

Cross over and slightly right to a gate with a bridleway sign, and continue along a track on the left-hand side of the field. This track is, I believe, called Marston Doles Lane. After a second field you arrive at a gate and a rare thing in these parts – a view! If you look to the right you should see Napton on the Hill with its distinctive windmill. Carry on down the hill to a gate, along a green lane, and then along the left-hand side of an arable field. Eventually, after a few more gates, the well-defined track becomes a green lane, which then becomes tarmacked as it passes Potash Farm, and leads down towards Marston Doles. At a junction go left (straight on), soon arriving at a T-junction, where you go right. Go over the canal bridge and left, through a gate and onto the Oxford Canal towpath. After, with luck, watching the canal-barges having fun with the locks, continue southish along the towpath (Remember! you need a British Waterways permit). At first the towpath is quite good, but there are some sections where it can be very narrow. Keep your eyes on the path and be careful not to go too close to the edge, otherwise

Oxford Canal at Marston Doles

you might have a nasty accident!

Leave the canal at the second bridge and enter the field on your right. This next section can be a little awkward, and could be very difficult in the wet. Cross the field in a general south-westerly direction, aiming for the radio mast in the distance. On the far side of the field you come to a gate, where you continue straight on across the next field along a definite track. Eventually you arrive at an old gate, followed by a short stretch of pasture and another gate. After crossing a further field you come to an overgrown corner, where there is a wooden bridge and a gate which leads into a green lane. Still aiming for the radio mast, continue along the lane for about 100m until it opens out into a field. At this point go left and due south, around the left-hand side of the field, shortly to arrive at a barn. Here you will probably be extremely relieved to find an excellent track and that the most difficult part of the route is now over. Follow the superb track, which climbs very gently up towards Wormleighton. This pretty little village has many attractive houses and the rather curious building, The Tower. Soon you arrive at the main road in the village, where you go left.

Follow the road for about one kilometre and then turn left for Priors Hardwick. After about another kilometre and just opposite the site of the medieval village of Stoneton, you will see the drive to Berryhill Farm on the right. Climb the steep little hill, admiring the view as you go, until you arrive at the farm. Go right, through a gate and follow a track around the edge of the field, to the back of the farm. Continue on the track along the left-hand side of a field and down to a line of trees, where you go left. Follow along the right-hand side of the field by the side of the trees, until you reach a gate which leads into an arable field. Things get slightly difficult here but if you continue on around the left-hand edge of the field, you soon come to a double gate which leads into a pasture. Go right and down to the end of the field, past a pool, to a double gate and onto a green lane. Follow this charming lane which does a sharp right and leads down to another gate and into another pasture. This is obviously an ancient route as the track continues on down between lines of old oaks and hawthorn. Soon you come to a gate, which is followed by a couple more pastures and eventually leads out onto a lane.

Go left and along the lane, soon to arrive at a crossroads. Our route goes right here, but it is well worth the effort of a detour through the very pretty village of Priors Hardwick, if only to visit the Butcher's Arms for quick refreshments (if you are in a fit state!). In any case, follow the road east out of the village for Priors Marston, which is a little over a kilometre away. When you arrive at the village, go left and then first right, for Hellidon. Climb up steeply out of the village and then go left at the top of the hill. Continue along the lane for a short distance, until you see a farm on the right, by the side of which is a track with a bridleway signpost. Follow this good, dirt track along the side of a couple of fields, eventually arriving at a gate. Continue straight on across a pasture and towards a farm. Follow the bridleway markers past the farm. Where the private drive goes right, you continue on and through a gate into an arable field. Follow along the left-hand edge of this and at the far end, go through a gap in the hedge and out onto a road, where you go left.

Just past a house, go left where there is a bridleway sign and follow the excellent track, with pleasant views, along the side of a large golf course. Eventually you come to a gate. Go through the gate and continue along the left-hand side of a field and down a tricky little descent. Follow the bridleway signpost along the edge of the next field, then turn right and go across the field on a good track towards a barn. Go past this to a gate, through which you turn right. After passing through another gate, the track leads you along the bottom of some woods. This takes you alongside the golf course and after a couple more gates, you come out onto a byway, where you go left. Follow this excellent track, which is a pure joy to ride and goes in an almost dead straight line, until finally bearing left.

Just around the corner you will see a bridleway signpost on the right. Follow this through a gate and along the left-hand side of a field on a reasonable track. After a short distance you will see a gate on the left, with a bridleway marker. Take this and continue along the right-hand side of a field for a couple of hundred metres. Turn right through another gate and then along the side of the next field to a further gate. Continue on through this and across the pasture towards Park Farm, after which you take the track which leads back to the main road at Shuckburgh and the start of the route.

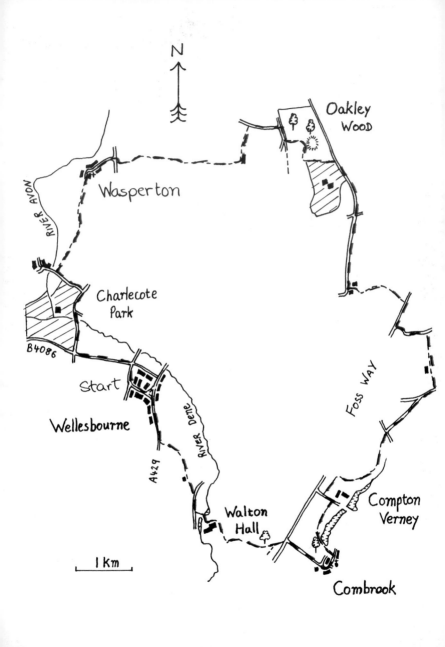

N

Oakley Wood

Wasperton

RIVER AVON

Charlecote Park

B4086

Start

Wellesbourne

A429

RIVER DENE

Walton Hall

Foss Way

Compton Verney

Combrook

1 Km

14.   Stratford-upon-Avon

Route Summary
Wellesbourne, Charlecote, Hampton Lucy, Wasperton, Oakley Wood, Little
Morrell, Lighthorne Rough, Compton Verney, Combrook, Walton Hall.

Details
Grade – moderate.
Time – 3 hrs.
Distance – 28km.
         off road – 15km.
         on road – 13km.
Terrain – parkland, fields and woods.
Surface – gravel and grass tracks, muddy in woods.
Start Grid Reference – SP 277551.
Maps – Stratford-upon-Avon & surrounding area L151.

Introduction
The landscape to the east of Stratford-upon-Avon is characterised by low
lying, gently rolling arable country. Within this lie neat little villages with
thatched cottages, well-ordered fields and scattered prosperous country
estates, of which there are a large number in Warwickshire. Most of the off
road riding on this route is on good bridleways and well-compacted tracks.
There are short sections which might cause difficulties, beside ploughed fields
for example, but these should be fairly easily overcome.

    The route starts at Wellesbourne and almost immediately passes the grand
house and grounds of Charlecote Park, now owned by the National Trust. The
off road riding starts at the village of Hampton Lucy, named after the Lucy
family who originally owned the Park, and passes through the quaint little
village of Wasperton. From here we go cross-country, mostly on farm tracks

and good bridleways, to Ashorne House and then via the Foss Way to Compton Verney. The off road riding here is either on good tracks or across parkland with only a short difficult section in a wood. After leaving the estate we pass through the pretty village of Combrook and then across the Foss Way again. The following section, to Walton Hall, probably presents the real challenge of the route, involving difficult fields and woods, but is well worth the effort. From Walton Hall we return to the start via a good track and the main road into Wellesbourne.

Route Description

Take the B4086 north-west out of Wellesbourne towards Stratford and after about 1km turn right onto the B4088 for Charlecote. Go past the main entrance to the hall (too early to stop for a cream tea unfortunately!) and take the first left for Hampton Lucy. Just before you reach the mill there is a bridleway on the right. Go through a gate, into a field and follow the bridleway along the left-hand boundary across to a gate. After going through this bear slightly left to another small gate and a bridge over Thelsford Brook. Go left over the bridge and then bear right on a raised path round past a new plantation to a good track. Take this, soon arriving at a small road which takes you into Wasperton. Follow the road through the village until you reach the main A429. Do a dogleg here (take care!) by going right and then left onto an excellent farm track. The track takes you up past the farm, then bears left. You, however, carry straight on along a grassy track by the side of a field. The track improves and eventually you come to a gate. Go through this and up towards Heathcote Farm. Turn left in front of the house, over a cattle grid and down a lane to the road. Go right at the road to a T-junction where you again go right.

After about 300m the road bears right and a track to Ashorne continues straight on. Do not follow this but take a narrower bridleway that goes east around the edge of Oakley Wood. Follow this past Ashorne Hill College until you arrive at a road, where you go right. After just over 2km you arrive at Little Morrell. Turn left down a drive (just before a right bend) and go past the farm, where you bear right and then left. After about 200m the track opens out into a field. Here you turn right and take a slightly less-defined track which follows the edge of the field and eventually leads round to a road – the Foss Way. Go right here, then left at the next junction for Lighthorne. Follow the road up and round past Bath Copse until you come to a track on the right for Far

The bridleway to Compton Verney

Westfields Farm. Go up this bridleway, through the gate at the farm (beware of the dogs) and down the drive to the road.

Turn right at the road and then fork next left down the hill to a T-junction with a track ahead. Go straight across and onto a good bridleway which eventually leads onto the Compton Verney estate via a gate. Ahead you will see the house of Compton Verney, designed by Robert Adam in 1760, together with its church and surrounded by the landscape of 'Capability' Brown. The lakes together with the bridge were considered to be one of Brown's most beautiful stretches of naturalised water. Go up the track, admiring the view and bear right. At the top of the rise turn right through a gate towards some farm buildings. Turn left past the farm and head straight for the lodge on the road. At the road, go left down the hill and near the bottom you will see a signpost for 'Park Farm' on the right. Go along this bridleway past the turning for Park Farm and then fork left through a gate by the side of a cattle grid and into a field. Trend left down the field on a vague track to a gate which enters the wood by the lake. This location provides another excellent view of the old Compton Verney estate and lakes. Go into the wood (this can be difficult in the wet) and out the other side via another small gate. Follow the track down to a hollow and up the other side to arrive in the village by a row of pretty little cottages. This is the estate village of Combrook, built to replace the original village which was demolished when the park of Compton Verney was created. Turn right through the village, eventually forking left uphill to the main road, the Foss Way, again.

Go left at the road, then immediately fork right and down a track. At the bottom the track bears left. You, however, continue straight on along the left-hand side of a field (with a ditch on your left) on an indefinite track which leads into a wood. This can present some problems, particularly in the summer when the crops are well-advanced, but persevere as this is only a short section. Follow the track through the wood (soft in places) and then cut across a field and up to (Thank God) a solid track at the top. Go left here and down to a gate, where you will have a good view of Walton Hall ahead. Continue along the track, through another gate, bear left by some new apartments and then continue past the 19th century hall and parish church. Follow the drive round, over the bridge and lakes to the road, where you go right. Take the second left turning along a track signposted 'The Old Rectory'. Continue past the houses, eventually arriving at the main A429 where you turn right (take care!) and return to the start in Wellesbourne.

The bridleway past Walton Hall

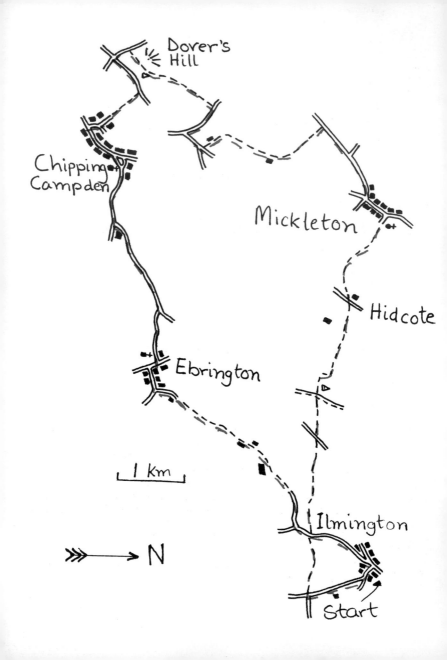

Dover's Hill

Chipping Campden

Mickleton

Hidcote

Ebrington

1 km

⋙ → N

Ilmington

Start

GLOUCESTERSHIRE

15. Chipping Campden and Hidcote

Route Summary
Ilmington, Foxcote, Ebrington, Chipping Campden, Dover's Hill, Dairy Hills, Mickleton, Kiftsgate Court, Hidcote Manor, Nebsworth, Ilmington.

Details
Grade – very difficult.
Time – 3 hrs.
Distance – 27km.
        off road – 15km.
        on road – 12km.
Terrain – hills.
Surface – good, well-drained hilly grass/pebble tracks.
Start Grid Reference – SP 213434.
Maps – Stratford-upon-Avon & surrounding area L151.

Introduction
The Ilmington Downs, as they are known locally, form the highest point in Warwickshire at a height of 259 metres above sea level. Situated in the far south-west of the county, they allude to an altogether different kind of terrain from that found in the rest of Warwickshire. Here you will find more than just a hint of the hilly Cotswold country to the south and, although separated from them, the downs can be considered as the northernmost outlier of the Cotswolds. The route starts in the charming village of Ilmington, climbs round the eastern flanks of the downs and drops down into Chipping Campden by way of Ebrington. From here, a stiff climb takes us up onto Dover's Hill escarpment, to be rewarded with fine panoramic views of the Vale of Eavesham. The hill derives its name from Robert Dover who in the early 1600s created the 'Cotswold Olympic Games' there. These games proved so

popular and boisterous that they had to be banned in the 19th century, due to riots in Chipping Campden. At any rate the hill is safe now and the bridleway provides a fun and sporting descent! The bridleway over Dairy Hills brings us to Mickleton, and then the hard work starts. An ever increasingly steep bridleway climbs up past Kiftsgate Court Garden and then Hidcote Manor and Gardens. Pretty flowers may not be your most important consideration at this stage, but at least the National Trust provide refreshments at Hidcote. Still more climbing takes us over the Ilmington Downs and then back home.

Route Description

Leave the charming little Cotswold village of Ilmington via the little road for Shipston, opposite the Red Lion pub. Shortly after leaving the village go right for Compton Scorpion and past Harolds Farm. At the junction of a road from the left, you go right, across a field and to a gate. Ascend the steep hill, eventually arriving at a gate, which leads onto a road. Resist the temptation to carry straight on, this is our return route, but go left and along the lane. After only 300m bear right and through a gate where it is signposted 'Foxcote House and Farm Only – Private Drive' – this is in fact a bridleway. The drive leads towards the very impressive early eighteenth century mansion, where we bear right and go downhill. Climb up past some houses and barns and continue straight on alongside an arable field on a good track. The track enters another field, bears left and down, then right at the bottom and up past some farm buildings. The track eventually becomes tarmacked and leads into another charming Cotswold village, Ebrington.

At the T-junction, go right and follow the main road through the little village, heading for Chipping Campden. After a couple of kilometres, turn right onto the B4035 and follow the one-way system into Chipping Campden. Go left onto the main street and where the main road bears left, continue straight on for Weston-sub-Edge. Take the next right past the church. The road bears round to the right, but we go left and up Hoo Lane, on the Cotswold Way. The tarmac gives out and becomes a track which climbs up Dover's Hill to a road. Here you go left and along to a crossroads. Turn right and go on up to the top and the Dover's Hill carpark on the right.

Dover's Hill has got to be one of the highlights of the trip, so have a picnic, enjoy the view and then prepare to have some fun! Go through the bridle gate along the Cotswold Way keeping to the boundary on the right-hand side. Follow this round to a gate and through this into a small wood. Follow the

The bridleway over Ilmington Downs

obvious track out onto open ground and then enjoy a rattling good descent to the road. At the road turn right, then first left and after about 400m you come to a T-junction. Ignore the roads and go left down a bridleway signposted 'Private Road'. Just after some farm buildings on the left there is a bridleway signpost on the right which takes you into the trees. This actually runs parallel to the road but is a lot more fun (and it is legal). The wood and track end at a gate, where you continue across the field straight ahead. Negotiate three more gates to eventually come to Middle Norton Farm. Cross the farm track (which actually leads to the road but is not a right of way) and aim in a leftish way past some woods to a small bridle gate on the far side of the field. This can be difficult in the wet and there is no clear indication of where the track goes. If and when you reach the gate, go through this and down the side of the field, eventually coming to the road previously mentioned.

At the road, go right and into Mickleton. Just before the church turn right, go up a lane and through a bridle gate between the graveyards. Cross the field, bearing right to another bridle gate and a stream. Follow the woods and stream to yet another gate and up the edge of the field to a small gate on the right. This takes you into the Kiftsgate Court Estate. Continue up an increasingly steep hill to reach a small road. After having a much needed rest, cross over the road and continue on up past the entrance and carpark of Hidcote Gardens (tea stop?) to a gravel track straight ahead. Follow this to the top of a hill and then a road. Cross over and follow the track down by the side of the field. Cycle through the wood, across another field and down to a small bridle gate in the far left-hand corner. Cross over the road and climb up a sandy track past some radio masts. Enjoy the view of the Midland plain to the north, and then continue through some woods and eventually down to the small road that we started out on. Turn left here and return to the village by a steep descent on road, but make sure your brakes are still working first!

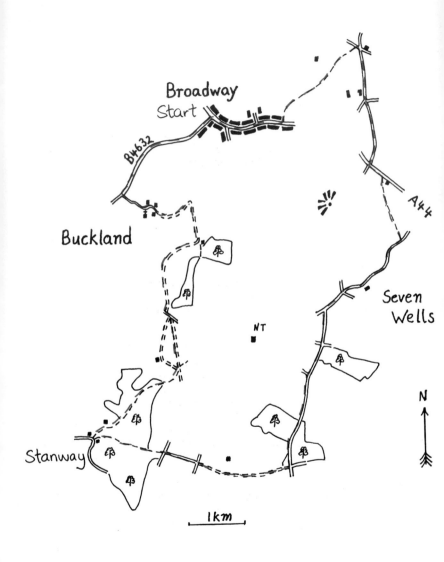

Broadway
Start

B4632

Buckland

A44

Seven Wells

NT

Stanway

N

1 km

16. Broadway

Route Summary
Broadway, Buckle Street, Ryknild Street, Taddington, Lidcombe Wood, Shenberrow Hill, Laverton Hill, Buckland, Broadway.

Details
Grade – very difficult.
Time – 3 hrs.
Distance – 27km.
          off road – 13km.
          on road – 14km.
Terrain – hills.
Surface – parkland, fields, woodland tracks and hardpack.
Start Grid Reference – SP 096375.
Maps – Worcester, The Malverns & surrounding area L150.

Introduction
The route starts in the centre of the picturesque little town of Broadway, which on a fine summer's day, and particularly at weekends, can be almost overrun by day trippers. The sight of a multi-coloured mountain biker at the end of a long hard day may cause some mild amusement amongst those less energetic! Fortunately, the route soon escapes the hustle and bustle of the town and climbs steeply via parkland up onto the Cotswold escarpment, from where there is a superb view to the west. The route tracks south, using a combination of quiet Cotswold lanes and a RUPP section of the Ryknild Street, an old Roman Road much fallen into disuse. After turning west down a pleasant little unclassified road the fun really starts.

    A superb descent through woods is followed by an energy-sapping climb back up onto Shenberrow Hill. The reward is an exhilarating ride along the crest of the hill on an excellent RUPP. The view to the west and north can be quite stunning on a clear day. Look out for the National Trust's Snowshill

Manor, a 15th century house and gardens well worth a visit, with an interesting museum of unusual collections. After about 4km, the track leads down into the sleepy village of Buckland and back to Broadway.

An alternative route for those who would prefer an almost completely off road experience is also possible. Starting at Buckland, climb east up the steep hill and follow the RUPP along the east side of Laverton Hill to Great Brockhampton Farm and then a T-junction. A right turn followed by a left will take you along a bridleway to a road junction where you turn left to Welshman's Hedge Wood. Here you can follow the bridleway through and along the side of the wood to arrive at a road, where a right turn will eventually bring you to the unclassified county road mentioned in the main route description. Here you follow the route back to Buckland via the woods down to Stanway or, if you want to make life somewhat easier, along the RUPP from Stanway Ash Wood and over Shenberrow and Laverton Hill. Total distance is about 15km, only 2km on road.

Route Description

Start in the centre of Broadway, heading east along the main A44. As the road begins to climb near the edge of the town, there is a lane on the left signposted 'Willersey and Saintbury Church'. Gratefully leave the noise of the town and follow the lane past some houses to a white bridle gate on the right, just where the track bears left. This is where the hard work begins! Cross the short stretch of field to a gap. Bear right to another gate and then left up the hill on the obvious grassy track. Go through another gate and continue along by the side of a new plantation to open ground. Bear right uphill and cross the parkland following the obvious grassy track. At the top left-hand corner is a gate in some trees, through which you continue on and up to a drive. Cross this and bear left to a gate.

The bridleway now weaves its way through trees and bushes at the bottom of the Golf Course. Resist the temptation to actually ride on the course, because not only is this illegal and possibly dangerous, it is also cheating! Continue along the good track (soft in places) until you arrive at a small lane, where you go right.

Turn right at the crossroads and climb uphill to a junction, where you go right (straight on) for Snowshill along the old Buckle Street. This lane is thought to be Neolithic in origin and the name may be derived from Saxon, meaning beacon, as the road traverses the tops of the hills. At the main A44 from Broadway go left (take care!). After only 300m turn right where there is a bridleway sign near a house. Pass through a gate and into a long, grassy field to another gate at the far end. Go through this and continue down along a narrow track by the side of the field to the bottom where it becomes wider. This is the old Roman Road, the Ryknild Street, which leads to a road where you go right. (The Ryknild Street does continue to Spring Hill House, but unfortunately is no longer a right of way.)

Follow the road up past Seven Wells and eventually bear left for Stow and Bourton on the Water. The lanes in this area are very quiet and on a fine day, the high plateau of the Cotswolds can be most pleasant. Go over a crossroads and downhill, continuing straight on where a road comes in from the right. Then climb uphill steadily towards some woods. Although this may not be the most challenging of biking, the rewards for this effort are soon to arrive.

As the road leaves the woods you will see a road on your left and on your right a track signposted 'Unsuitable for Motors' (SP 104314). Go right and down past the edge of the wood on this excellent track. This crosses a stream at Dirty Bridge and then continues up to a road junction. Carry straight on up a narrow lane for Stanway towards the woods at the top and another junction. At this point it would be possible to go right where it is signposted 'Unsuitable for Motors' to join our route at a later stage. This would, however, make life far too easy and would also miss one of the delights of the route! Continue straight on into the wood, following a bridle signpost, to arrive at a large gate which is the entrance to the Stanway Estate. There now follows a rattling good decent through the woods on excellent track, with many bumps and a few rocks, all the way to the bottom. Resist any temptation to branch left or right, as these are not rights of way, but continue down to eventually arrive at some houses.

Unfortunately, all good things come to an end and usually they have to be paid for! Just before you reach the road there is a narrow lane which doubles back up to your right. Although this starts off quite steep and can be very soft, it soon levels out. This is the start of a reasonably gentle but interesting little climb all the way back up onto the Cotswold plateau. The scenery here is quite delightful and the climbing never too hard to spoil the fun — in fact, this is what off road biking is all about. The track widens and follows the edge of the wood to arrive at a pool. Continue straight on following the bridleway signpost, past a hidden reservoir and noisy pumps (if running) and on uphill. The track climbs steadily and then finally becomes short and steep, arriving at the edge of the woods by a farm. Bear left along the edge of the woods and where the track bears right and leaves the woods (footpath only), you carry straight on through a small gate and into a small field. Cross this diagonally right to a green gate. Cross a similar field to another green gate and onto a large track. This is in fact a RUPP which follows the top of Shenberrow Hill.

Go left and follow the excellent track, admiring the views, until you arrive at a gate which leads onto a lane. Go left for about 100m or so until you see a signpost on your right saying 'Cotswold Way'. Follow this, through a gate and again along the RUPP with an excellent view of Broadway ahead. The track goes downhill, past a bridleway on the left and down to a gate with a blue bridleway marker.

Continue along the firm track, through another gate with a marker, to arrive at a barn. This is in fact the junction of another RUPP. We go left through a gate and along a solid track. After a while the track bears round to the left, becomes tarmacked and quicky descends into the very pretty village of Buckland. Carry on through the village to the main B4632 where you turn right and return to the start in Broadway.

112

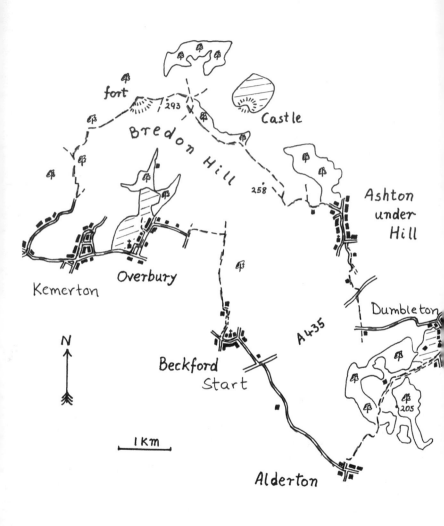

fort

293

Bredon Hill

Castle

258

Ashton
under
Hill

Kemerton

Overbury

Dumbleton

A435

Beckford
Start

205

N

1 Km

Alderton

WORCESTERSHIRE

17. Bredon and Dumbleton

Route Summary
Beckford, Alderton, Dumbleton, Ashton under Hill, Bredon Hill, Kemerton, Overbury, Beckford.

Details
Grade – very difficult.
Time – 4 hrs.
Distance – 30 km.
        off road – 18km.
        on road – 12km.
Terrain – hills.
Surface – mostly good gravel tracks.
Start Grid Reference – SO 976357.
Maps – Worcester, The Malverns & surrounding area L150.

Introduction
Bredon Hill, situated in the county of Hereford and Worcester, is what is geologically called an outlier. Here the Cotswold limestone beds have been raised and folded by prehistoric forces and then eroded over the passage of time. The result is a hill that presents two different facets. To the south, the land slopes away gently along the plane of the beds, whilst the northern flank of the hill is much steeper. The hill is almost 1000ft high and, although separate, is considered to be part of the Cotswolds. There are numerous bridleways, footpaths and old tracks crossing the hill, many in excellent condition. This route links with the smaller but even prettier hills of Alderton and Dumbleton to the south-east, and although this involves a little riding on small lanes, the excursion is well worthwhile. For those who prefer an almost

complete off road experience it is possible to contrive a route that climbs and descends Bredon Hill three times, via Ashton under Hill, Elmley Castle, Kemerton and Overbury. This involves over 2000ft of climbing, which is probably a record for mountain biking in the Midlands!

Route Description

Starting by the church in the centre of the village of Beckford, go east and follow the road round to the right, soon arriving at the main A435. Taking care, do a dogleg left, then right for Alderton. This quiet lane soon takes you away from the noise and after a couple of kilometres you arrive at the village itself. As you enter the village, just before the Gardeners Arms pub, there is a track with a bridleway signpost on the left. Follow this out of the village and up the side of a couple of fields towards the woods. Go through a gate and straight on into the woods, ignoring the tracks to the left and right. Climb up the steep track through some very pretty woods, which can also be quite difficult after a period of wet. At the top you arrive at a track where you go left to a large gate. This bridleway takes you down past Hill Farm to the village of Dumbleton. The views at this point are quite spectacular, but take care – watch your speed as you descend, as the track has speed bumps which can take you by surprise (we speak from painful experience!). Follow the track down past Dumbleton Hall on the left, with its lake, to the main gate. Go left, along the lane and then left again into the village. Follow the road through the village, bearing left at the end. After a little over a kilometre you will see a grassy bridleway on your right opposite a house. Go through the large gates and follow the track to the main road again.

At the main road go right and then immediately left through a small gate, where there is a bridleway signpost. Follow this track down to the drive of a caravan site and on to the reception(!). Bear right and go around the back of the site where there is a blue waymarker. The track takes you to a small gate, through which you go right, along the edge of a field on a good track, arriving eventually at a lane. Follow Back Lane into the village of Ashton under Hill, where you go left and then right for Elmley Castle. Continue north on the main street – stop off at the Star pub if you are in need of refreshments – then on up the village until you see Cottons Lane on the left. This tarmacked lane soon becomes a bridleway and enters some trees. Go through a gate, and climb up past a farm to another gate. Climb more steeply on a rocky track to yet another gate and then to a division of tracks. Go left, through a gate and up the right-hand side of the field. The track is ill-defined but at the top you join a definite track, where you go left. This takes you through a gate and round the hill to the right. Just around the corner the track divides and you continue straight on (right), following the bridleway signpost indicating that you are on the Wychavon Way. At the top is a gate through which you turn right and follow the edge of an arable field round to the left. This excellent track climbs very gently now, so take time to admire the view to the south-east of the Cotswolds and closer to hand, Dumbleton Hill.

Continue climbing along the good track, go through a gate and cycle alongside another arable field. Further on still there are fine views on your right of the Vale of Evesham and of Evesham itself. Go through another gate and continue alongside trees. This excellent track passes near a communications tower and eventually you will see a bridle gate which enters a wood. (For those who like to spice things up a little, it is possible to take this track down into the wood, turn sharp left as you leave the wood and then return to the original route, after a stiff little hill climb.) Continue straight on, eventually arriving at a copse on the left and a gate. The steep nature of the northern flank of Bredon Hill now becomes apparent. Carrying straight on along the right-hand side of grazing land we arrive at Bredon Hill fort. Keep to the wall on the right (the fort itself is NOT a right of way for bikes), but notice the double ditch that surrounds the fort. When the Iron Age fort was excavated, apparently the mutilated bodies of fifty men were discovered. These last defenders of the fort had not been buried, but had presumably been left where they fell. As you follow the wall round to the left you pass the Banbury Stone, considered by some to be a Druid sacrificial stone, and then a tower called Parsons Folly. The track passes the double ditch again, goes through a gate and starts to descend towards some woods.

Enter the deciduous wood via a gate and then continue by the side of the woods on an excellent sandy track with good views to the south. Eventually you arrive at a small gate, through which you turn left and go down the left-hand side of a couple of fields. Notice the superb view of the Malvern Hills on the right. Continue downhill and bear left past the end of the copse and onto an obvious track. Follow the track down past another clump of trees and bear left to a gate. Follow the gravel track right and downhill. Eventually the track becomes tarmacked and bears right, continuing down to the village of Lower Westmancote.

In the village you arrive at a T-junction, where you go left for Kemerton and

Looking towards Dumbleton Hill from Bredon Hill

Overbury. Although not strictly necessary, a detour north through the village of Kemerton is well worthwhile, as the village is particularly attractive. On arriving at Overbury take the first left, up past the church and round to the main street, where you go left. (As you climb uphill note the entrance to Overbury Park on your left, which is in fact a bridleway which will take you back up to the top of Bredon Hill.) Carry on up to the top of the village and turn first right. Follow the lane out of the village and where the lane goes sharp right, you turn left (east) up a gravel track. Soon the track splits and you bear right, go over a small stream and climb the hill. At the top of the climb you arrive at a junction. Go right and follow the track downhill to a farm. Go left through the farmyard and then right and onto a tarmacked lane, which takes you down to the village of Beckford. At the junction go left for Alderton and back to the start of the route.

The bridleway down to Westmancote

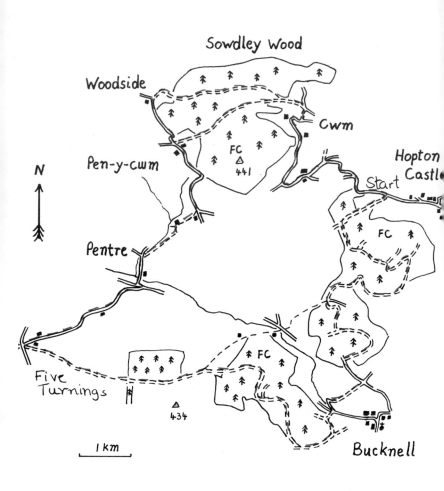

Sowdley Wood

Woodside

Cwm

Hopton
Castle

Pen-y-cwm

N

FC
△
441

Start

FC

Pentre

△

Five
Turnings

FC

△
434

1 km

Bucknell

SHROPSHIRE

18. Hopton Castle

Route Summary
Hopton Titterhill, Cwm, Sowdley Wood, Woodside, Pentre, Five Turnings, Stow Hill, Bucknell Wood, Bucknell Hill, Hopton Titterhill.

Details
Grade – severe.
Time – 4 hrs.
Distance – 35km.
        off road – 22km.
        on road – 13km.
Terrain – very hilly, wooded.
Surface – mostly forestry tracks and green lanes.
Start Grid Reference – SO 348778.
Maps – Ludlow, Wenlock Edge & surrounding area L137.

Introduction
This challenging route is located around the mountain bike trails at Hopton Castle, situated just eight miles west of Craven Arms and close to the Shropshire-Hereford border. The Forestry Commission, with their very enlightened attitude, have devised a number of trails within Hopton Wood specifically for mountain bikers. The woods occupy about 860 acres and there are trails to suit all abilities. Trails are marked with numbered posts and there is an excellent guide available from the Forestry Commission. For those with a more adventurous nature, however, this route is presented as an alternative.

    The area is characterised by some quite respectable hills, interleaved with little country lanes that have all but fallen into disuse. Although classified as county maintained roads, it appears that some of them have seen little maintenance for many a year! This is particularly the case around Llanadevy and Cwm, allowing a very pleasant link between Hopton Titterhill and the Forestry Commission Sowdley Wood. Small roads, followed by a fun bridleway with superb views, bring us to Pentre and then on to Five Turnings. Here we take the bridleway over Stow Hill (difficult in places) and enjoy a relaxing descent through Bucknell Wood, also owned by the Forestry Commission. A stiff little climb up Bucknell Hill returns us to the Hopton Wood bike trails, where we can take any route of our choice, depending on how much energy is left!

Route Description

The route starts at the forestry carpark at Hopton Titterhill. Leave the delights of Hopton Woods behind for later and head back down the track to the road. Turn left here and climb steadily through trees, then fork right for Llanhowell. Soon you arrive at a crossroads on a bend. Straight on takes you to the farm, but the status of the track beyond is in dispute, so go left and uphill. The barely maintained lane climbs up through trees, past a farm, to arrive at a T-junction, where you go right. After about 1km, this narrow and overgrown lane takes you down past a trout farm at Cwm and then uphill again. Take the next left up a very disused road, which is more off road than on. At the top go left and through a gate and up a grassy track, which is supposed to be a county maintained road! This can be rather overgrown later on in the season, but persevere as at the top is another gate, after which the track gets a little easier. Follow this up the side of the wood and after about 100m, you will see a track which enters the wood. Here you have a choice. The first option is to continue straight on along the track by the side of the wood. This shortly brings you to a gate, the other side of which is a section of very overgrown track, about 200m or so. Once past this the going gets easier (and prettier) and eventually you join a main forestry track which takes you down to the crossroads near Pen-y-cwm. Alternatively, the second option is to go right and follow the narrow track through the wood, dodging tree stumps, low branches and the like. Soon the track opens out and you can then enjoy a relaxing run down through Sowdley Wood on the main forestry track. Unfortunately, all good things come to an end and eventually you arrive at a road at Woodend. Here you continue straight on (left) and up a very steep hill to arrive at the same crossroads near Pen-y-cwm. The choice is very simple: an easy way down through the wood and then steep climb back up, or fight your way through the gorse along the county 'maintained' road!

122

The county maintained road down to Pen-y-cwm

Either way, go straight on at the crossroads and continue south-east along the road past Pen-y-cwm farm and round the Fiddler's Elbow. Soon there is a junction where the road bears left, but you go right and through a gate just before a barn. Go through a second gate and then follow the obvious track, with fine views, which goes downhill and arrives at a farm. Turn left here and go down to a gate. On your left you will see two gates. Take the one on the left and follow a steep track up the right-hand side of the field to another gate on the right. A steep and slightly tricky descent then follows, which soon brings you to a cottage. After negotiating a few more gates and enjoying a very pleasant ride alongside a stream, you arrive at a road. Go left here and down to Pentre. At the T-junction turn left and then, very soon, sharp right and up the road for 'Five Turnings'.

The road climbs steeply, then more gently arriving after approx. 2½km at the main road at Five Turnings. Double back left and past a house, following an excellent track, which is a bridleway, up Stow Hill. As you climb, the track becomes narrower, until you reach a gate. The track, which is now a RUPP, continues alongside an arable field. This part can be difficult, depending on the time of year, and may need to be walked. Continue through another couple of gates and then along the edge of a wood. The track climbs gently until, at the end of the wood, it starts to descend towards Bucknell Wood. About ½km after leaving the end of the wood the track arrives at a gate. The track left continues on the RUPP down to the river. Straight on takes you into Bucknell Wood. However, the short section of track which takes you into the Forestry Commission wood is a private track. Mr Williams of Vron Farm has kindly given permission to use this track across his land. **Keep to the permissive track and close all gates after you.** Once in the wood follow the major Forestry Commission track, which provides a fun descent and leads to the valley bottom. Continue on the track around the base of the hill, ignoring the track to Bucknell, and then go right at the end of the wood to the road.

On the other side of the road is a footbridge over the River Redlake. Cross this or ford the river and then go left up a small lane. This leads to a gate by a house and then does a sharp right uphill and past the back of the house. The road becomes grass and a delightful little green track with a good view back down to Bucknell. After passing through some gates, the track leads onto a lane. Here the route turns left and climbs up to Bucknell Hill. However, this section is a footpath. Please dismount and walk up this short stretch until you reach the wood (a good excuse to avoid the hill climb). At the top is an

Towards Bucknell Hill

entrance to the Hopton Titterhill and Bucknell Hill Forestry Commission woods and bike trails. As the Forestry Commission particularly welcome mountain bikes here, you can basically go where you like. For those tired after a hard day there is an easy track around the east of Bucknell Hill to the junction above Meeroak Farm. Continue roughly east and then zigzag back over the top of Hopton Titterhill and down to the carpark.

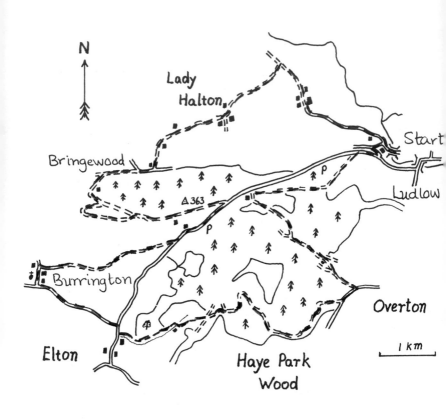

19. Ludlow

Route Summary
Ludlow, Priors Halton, Lady Halton, Deepwood, Gorsty, Monstay Rough, Burrington, Elton Hall, Haye Park Wood, Mary Knoll Valley and House, Upper Evens, Ludlow.

Details
Grade – very difficult.
Time – 3½ hrs.
Distance – 31km.
        off road – 24km.
        on road – 7km.
Terrain – hilly.
Surface – mostly forestry tracks, some field bridleways.
Start Grid Reference – SO 507744.
Maps – Ludlow, Wenlock Edge & surrounding area L137.

Introduction
Ludlow is said to be one of the most charming country towns in England. The well-preserved castle looks particularly grand when seen from Whitcliffe across the River Teme, and this is where our route starts. The extensive woods to the west of Ludlow form part of the Forestry Commission Mortimer Forest, an area well-known to local mountain bike enthusiasts, as well as to walkers. The Commission have created waymarked walks of varying difficulty, but fortunately for us, they also have an enlightened attitude towards mountain bikers! At the time of going to print, mountain bikers were allowed to bike almost anywhere, provided they kept clear of the waymarked walks, kept their speed down and respected other users of the forest. With such freedom to roam it is possible to create any number of routes, but it is a good idea to call at the Whitcliffe visitors centre to see if there are any temporary restrictions in force.

    One problem with all forestry, however, is that it can be very easy to get lost!

Also, forestry routes can get a little monotonous at times. With this route, I have tried to incorporate a little variety by including sections outside the forest. The route warms up with an easy excursion north via the Haltons, followed by a stiff climb up into Bringewood, with superb views as a reward. An easy run down into Burrington and across to Elton, is followed by more climbing and then a swift descent into Haye Park. From there the bridleway up Mary Knoll Valley is taken, with more fine views, and then back to Ludlow. Be prepared for a little leg work!

Route Description

Leave Ludlow via the Dinham Bridge. Just as the lane starts to climb, go right and straight ahead, where it is signposted for the Cliff Hotel. Unfortunately, it is too soon to stop for a drink, so continue north-west along the lane for Priors Halton. This little lane provides an excellent view of the forest on your left, a glimpse of things to come. At the farm, continue straight on where it is signposted 'Private – No Through Road' – this is in fact a bridleway. After going past a gate you enter the Oakly Park estate. About 300m along the tree-lined drive you will see another tarmac track on the left. Follow this through Lady Halton, where it becomes a gravel track, and on up towards the forest. After approx. 2½km the track arrives at a lane at Brick House, where you go right. After 300m the lane bears to the right, but you continue straight on, into Deep Wood.

Follow along the edge of the wood, ignoring the first major left. After about ½km, just past a little stream, fork left and up a steep grassy track. Push and pant your way up this testing little climb, to arrive at a rather strange building on your left. This in fact was built by the Birmingham Corporation Water Board and is part of the Elan Valley supply, which is of such importance to the folk of Birmingham. Continue on up through the trees, which brings you out onto a forestry track, where you go right and uphill. The track zigzags its way uphill and then begins to level out. About 200m after the last bend (look out for the fine view of Downton Castle) you double back right. Shortly this brings you to the edge of the Forestry Commission land and you bear left and follow the boundary uphill. This is fun biking and as you climb a superb vista opens out before you. Continue uphill until, at the top (339m), there is a seat. Stop here and have a rest because the view, on a good day, is special! To the west you can see the hills of Wales and the border lands, whilst south and east is a fine view of the rest of the forest, which you shall shortly be visiting.

128

Lower Whitcliffe from Priors Halton

Suitably refreshed, continue downhill to join a main forestry track from the left. Follow this down and along the edge of Bringewood, eventually reaching Gorsty. At the road, go right and downhill. After a little over a kilometre, just past a house, there is a track on the right. Follow this, through a gate, and on through Monstay Rough. This delightful little track winds its way down through Long Larches (Forestry Commission) and arrives at Burrington, where you go left.

Follow the lane out of the sleepy little hamlet to a T-junction, where the route goes left. A couple of kilometres along this lane brings you to the Wigmore road. Turn right almost immediately to Elton Hall. Just before the Hall is a bridleway on the left, with a very curious little hen-house(?) in the neighbouring field. Follow the bridleway up the left-hand side of the field, bearing right onto a more definite track, and into trees. The track climbs steadily up beside a stream, but is sometimes poorly defined. This takes you through a couple of fields, a wood and finally out into a large field.

Continue to climb until you see a bridge over the stream and a gate on the right. Go through this (barn on your right) and then follow the track uphill and to the left. Again, the track disappears but continue straight on until you see a gate on the right, which is the entrance to Brush Wood. This leads onto a track, where you go left and then immediately right, and uphill into the wood. This particular track can be a little rutted and soft at times. Soon you arrive at the top and emerge onto a large forestry track. Go right here and continue straight on, following the main track as it zigzags its way down, eventually arriving at some pools. Keep left here and follow the main track, which contours around the hill, to arrive finally at Haye Park carpark and the road.

Go left onto the road and down towards Overton. As the road bears right, you go left and along the main track up Mary Knoll Valley. About 100m after the signpost telling you that you are in Sunny Dingle Wood, fork right and up the hill past the cottage of the same name. Just past this, the main track does a hairpin right, but you continue straight on along a dirt track. A couple of hundred metres after a pool, the track bears left over the stream, but you carry on along a smaller track. Shortly after, you arrive at a gate which advertises that you are entering private woods, the Mary Knoll conservation area, so keep to the track. After another gate, you continue to climb up across a large field used for grazing (good views), and arrive at Mary Knoll House. Go past the house, through a gate into a field, immediately right and through another gate by a barn. Follow the right-hand edge of the field up to another gate and into the

The end of the day!

woods. Continue along the side of the wood and basically straight ahead, ignoring any tracks to the left or right. After passing the Whitcliffe visitors centre, the track gets narrow and quite technical in places. This is impossible to ride up, but the little drop-offs are quite fun on the way down. Make sure you have got your helmet on and take it easy! Too soon you arrive at the road where you go right. A first left and a hairpin bring you back down to the Dinham bridge and into Ludlow.

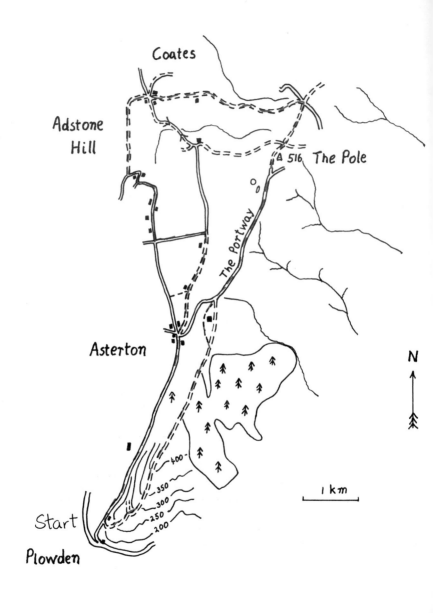

Coates

Adstone Hill

The Pole

▲ 516

The Portway

Asterton

Start

Plowden

N

1 km

400
350
300
250
200

20. The Long Mynd

Route Summary
Plowden, The Port Way, Pole Bank, Coates, Adstone Hill, Prolley Moor, Asterton, Plowden.

Details
Grade – difficult.
Time – 3 hrs.
Distance – 23km.
        off road – 13km.
        on road – 10km.
Terrain – a big hill!
Surface – moorland tracks, grassy and rocky.
Start Grid Reference – SO 384878.
Maps – Ludlow, Wenlock Edge & surrounding area L137.

Introduction
The Long Mynd is a justifiably popular hill and has been so since Victorian times. The hill runs approximately north-south and presents a different impression, depending upon your viewpoint. As one approaches along the main A49 from Shrewsbury, the hill takes on the appearance of a rather low raised mass of moorland, outshone by the more impressive Caer Caradoc Hills to the east. Not until the hill is approached more closely, via the Strettons, does the broken nature of the eastern side become more apparent. Here, the deep hollows which cut the eastern flank of the hill, called batches, are threaded by rivers and waterfalls. It is easy to see why the Victorians found Carding Mill Valley so fascinating, and it is still a popular tourist spot today. The western flank presents an altogether more different aspect. Here the hill appears long, smooth and steep-sided, and has a very remote feel to it. The

villages on this side of the hill are quiet, unspoilt and the lanes almost deserted to the point of being disused.

What few descriptions there are of mountain biking on the Mynd generally start on the eastern side of the hill. For example, it is possible to start at Church Stretton, travel south via Little Stretton and Minton to the main A489 road. By going west to Plowden the Portway can be joined – an ancient track which runs the length of the Mynd. This can be climbed and a return journey made south-east via Minton Batch, Carding Mill Valley, or even Robin Hood's Butts down to All Stretton. Interesting though these routes are they suffer from the disadvantage of having to use the main road through the Strettons, with all the hustle and bustle that is associated with these villages. As mountain biking is all about trying to 'get away from it all', this route is presented as an alternative. A traverse of the top is made from Plowden via the Portway to Pole Bank, the highest point on the Mynd. The return is then made via an exhilarating descent to the almost isolated community of Coates, and then via small lanes and disused county roads over Adstone Hill and along the western flank of the Mynd back to the start.

Route Description

Park your car somewhere along the road between Asterton and Plowden, and head south on the delightful little lane towards Plowden. Just after passing some cottages on the left you arrive at a cattle grid where you bear left through a bridle gate. This is marked with a bridleway marker and also a little badge (with a galloping horse) informing you that you are on the Jack Mytton Way. This also happens to be the start of the Portway which stretches from end to end of the Long Mynd. Gird up your loins, as the hard part is about to start!

The track bears left and then climbs steeply up the hill, to arrive at an enclosure with a couple of gates. Almost immediately you will see that the view to the west and south begins to open up. This is just as well as you will probably need to stop and admire it on several occasions during the climb. Follow the bridleway markers through the gates and on uphill along a definite track. After passing through another gate, bear slightly left and continue on a less defined track to arrive at a gate in the boundary on your left. The track improves and shortly the gradient eases off to reveal the panorama of the Long Mynd stretching out before you to the north. All the effort of the hill climb now seems worthwhile as you gently climb The Mynd, following a green track with heather and bracken on either side. If you are lucky you might even spy a

134

buzzard or two.

After a while you will see a notice on your right informing you that the bridleway that you are on is about to cross an airfield, and that you are to watch out for gliders! This might cause some trepidation were it not for the fact that 100m further on is another notice which invites you to take a permissive path around the edge of the airfield. As this provides excellent views of the western side of the Mynd, and is also a great deal safer than having a confrontation with a glider or its towing cable, there is not really much of a contest. Take the Starboardway, as the track is called, left and follow the little white posts. Eventually the track passes behind the gliding club buildings and to a road.

Take a right turn and continue north along the road, following the route of the old Portway. At weekends this small road can get quite busy, with sightseers enjoying the steep ride over the Mynd and also watching gliders, hang-gliders and even parapenters taking advantage of the prevailing south-westerly breeze. Fortunately, although this is likely to be the busiest part of the route, the views are ample compensation. After a couple of kilometres, just past an enclosure of trees, you will see a track and bridleway marker on the left. Jack Mytton has been this way as well! This good track rises up gently to the summit of The Pole, the highest point on the Long Mynd at 1696ft. Take a rest at the trig point and enjoy the view with the aid of the orientation plate. Apparently, on a clear day, it is even possible to see Snowdon and Cader Idris. At any rate, the views of the Caradoc Hills to the east and the Stiperstones and Wales to the west can be quite superb. Suitably refreshed, we now begin our long descent. Continue along the track, over a little rise and down to the road.

At the road there is a choice. Those who started in Church Stretton could continue straight across the road and along a track which soon brings you to Robin Hood's Butts (what was he doing over here!?). A right turn down a bridleway here will bring you to a road, which leads down Plush Hill and into All Stretton. Forsaking the hustle and bustle of the east side of the Mynd, however, our route goes left along the road for a short distance, and then bears left down a track. This pleasant county road, which is no more than a stony track, descends gently, rises a little, and then descends more steeply to a gate. The well-defined track continues alongside trees, through a couple of gates and down the left-hand side of fields. To your left you now have an excellent view of the wide expanse of the Long Mynd and you might find it hard to believe that you have just biked over this not inconsiderable hill. The track descends into the little hamlet of Coates.

Here you have a choice of routes for the return to Plowden. One possibility is to go left at Coates, through a gate and along the county road, which is little more than a track, to Medlicott. From there you can follow the road and then the track along the base of the Long Mynd to Asterton and finally, Plowden. Our route, however, bears right past some cottages and over a cattle grid, and then immediately left and up to a gate. Continue on through this up the left-hand side of a field on a track which is in fact a county road. At the top the track bears left through a couple of gates and then slowly climbs Adstone Hill, little more than a mound in comparison to the Long Mynd. Soon you reach the top and then descend to a gate. The old grassy track continues between lines of trees and after a sweeping descent, you arrive at a lane.

Follow the gated lane left and down through Adstone. After a sharp left you descend (do not go too fast, there is a gate at the bottom!) and pass by a couple of farms, to reach a crossroads. Straight on will lead to Asterton, but we go left and uphill for Medlicott. The road climbs gently towards the Mynd and, at such a late stage in the route, may seem a little hard on the legs. The benefits of this last little effort are soon revealed however. At the top of the road there is a T-junction. A right turn here takes you along a lane, past a farm, through a couple of gates and along a county 'road'. This delightful old lane winds its way along the foot of the Long Mynd. Enclosed by trees, it sometimes thinks it is a stream, but rarely becomes too boggy, due to the underlying rock. After going through a gate and on to more open ground, the track descends to Asterton. A left turn in the hamlet will then take you along the road and back to Plowden.

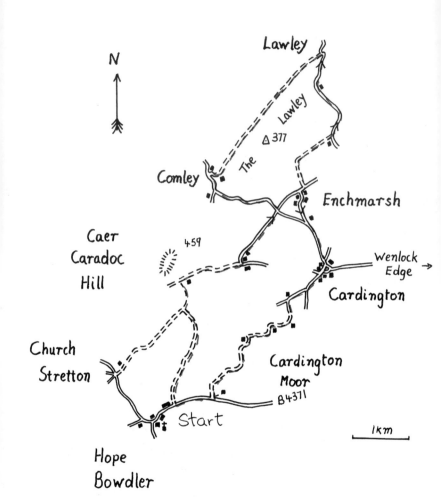

N

Lawley

The Lawley

△ 377

Comley

Enchmarsh

Caer
Caradoc
Hill

459

Wenlock
Edge →

Cardington

Church
Stretton

Cardington
Moor

B4371

Start

1km

Hope
Bowdler

21. Hope Bowdler

Route Summary
Hope Bowdler, Cardington Moor, Cardington, Enchmarsh, Hoar Edge, The Lawley, Willstone, Hope Bowdler Hill.

Details
Grade – moderate (tricky sections).
Time – 2½ hrs.
Distance – 20km.
        off road – 11km.
        on road – 9km.
Terrain – hilly.
Surface – grass and stony tracks.
Start Grid Reference – SO 478927.
Maps – Ludlow, Wenlock Edge & surrounding area L137.

Introduction
This varied and interesting little route is based around the Caer Caradoc Hills to the east of the Long Mynd. Seen from the latter, this curious chain of hills presents a striking profile, having more in common with the Welsh hills to the west than the low land of the Midlands to the east. The Caradoc Hills consist of The Lawley, a sort of smaller but steeper sided version of the Long Mynd, Caer Caradoc, Helmeth, Hazler, Ragleth and Hope Bowdler Hills. Although paths cross these hills, unfortunately, many of them are footpaths and therefore a no-go area for mountain bikes. It is possible, however, by linking small country lanes and bridleways to produce an interesting route that gives something of the flavour of the area.

    Although most of the route is very straightforward there are some steep and rocky sections which can present a little test of skill. For those requiring a more adventurous route it should be possible to link, via small lanes, with Wenlock Edge to the east, and this has been indicated on the sketch map.

Route Description

The route starts on the B4731 from Church Stretton to Much Wenlock, where there are a couple of parking places just past the village of Hope Bowdler. Go east along the road until you see Woodgate Cottage on your left. The bridleway, according to the OS map, starts at the beginning of the drive and bears left to a gate which leads onto a lane. Most people, however, seem to take the lane from the road just before the drive, even though it is not strictly a right of way. Climb steadily up the stony track, which levels off and bears right. After a gate the track descends steeply to a stream, with lots of loose scree and boulders to test your nerve and skill. It then climbs equally steeply up the other side.

After a cattle grid the terrain eases and the track contours around the hill to Middle Hill Farm. Descend past the farm and hairpin right and climb steadily back up. Shortly after the track does a sharp left and becomes concrete which then gives way to tarmac. Descend past some farms to arrive at a road, where we go left for Cardington.

Very soon you arrive at the village – but just as you enter look out for the rather interesting Brook House on your left, which has a splendid half-timbered entrance and a plaque with the date, 1574 RO over the door. Follow the main road through the village, or make a detour right by St James' Church and The Royal Oak pub, until you come to a T-junction, where you turn left. Soon after you fork left for Leebotwood and follow the lane out of the village. After about ½km the road bears left but you fork right and continue climbing up a narrow lane. This takes you up to the little hamlet of Enchmarsh. Fortunately, this is a quiet little lane, so it is quite permissible to get off and push if you need to! Follow the lane through Enchmarsh to arrive at a T-junction. Go right and then very soon, left up a gravel track.

The track climbs gently, passing several old abandoned cars. The last time I biked past this spot the cars seemed to be used as kennels for several ferocious sounding sheep dogs. Fortunately, the dogs were well-tethered so their barking was only slightly intimidating. Soon the track bears right to reveal an impressive view of The Lawley, a long steep-sided hill. The track descends steadily along Hoar Edge, with several boulders and rocks to provide sport. After about ½km it reaches a road, where you go left and down the hill. Follow

140

One way of getting up Hope Bowdler Hill

the road across the valley towards The Lawley, where it does a right turn, descends and bears left around the foot of the hill.

Just as the road does a hairpin right you will see a track on the left, which is a bridleway. Follow this good track past The Well House and along the base of the hill. This delightful track provides a good view towards the Long Mynd and later on, an impressive view of Caer Caradoc Hill. Apart from a few short sections where it can become rutted, the track is usually in excellent condition. After approx. 3km you arrive at a gate where you take the right-hand track down to the road. Go left and keep left at a fork near Comley, climbing steadily up past Broadstone to the junction near Enchmarsh. Turn right and climb up Folly Bank and then descend into Willstone.

As the road does a sharp left in Willstone, turn right up a broad dirt track, signposted 'Caer Caradoc Hill'. The track climbs steeply and then switchbacks along the southern flank of the hill. Just past the remains of Cwms Cottage and a copse is a bridleway on the left. This ill-defined track contours around the eastern flank of a hillock and then, on a better track, rises up to a bridle gate. After passing through this, bear left along a grassy track which starts to climb up Hope Bowdler Hill. Although rideable at first the track soon becomes too steep and it is better to dismount rather than churn up the turf and cause irreparable damage (to the ground and yourself!). After a short push the terrain eases off and it now becomes possible to bike over the hill. Descend the main broad grassy track with splendid views all around. Eventually, the track steepens and after passing through a gate, continues on down to the road and back to Hope Bowdler and the start. A very pleasant and interesting little route.

Appendix

Here are a few useful addresses:

County Councils –

Gloucestershire County Council, Cotswold Warden Office, County Planning Dept, Shire Hall, Gloucester, GL1 2TN.

Hereford & Worcester County Council, The Countryside Officer, County Hall, Spetchley Road, Worcester, WR5 2NP.

Leicestershire County Council, Countryside Section, Planning & Transportation Dept, County Hall, Glenfield, LE3 8RJ.

Northants County Council, Country Services, Countryside Centre, 9 Guildhall Road, Northampton, NN1 1DP.

Shropshire County Council, Countryside Service, Churchill Building, Radbrook Road, Shrewsbury, SY3 9BJ.

Staffordshire County Council, Countryside Access Officer, Martin Street, Stafford, ST16 2LE.

Warwickshire County Council, Countryside Services Group, Shire Hall, Warwick, CV34 4SX.

Forestry Commission –
Northants Forest District, Top Lodge, Fineshade, Nr Corby, NN17 3BB.

Marches Forest District, Whitcliffe, Ludlow, Shropshire, SY8 2HD.

Midlands Forest District, Lady Hill, Birches Valley, Rugeley, Staffs, WS15 2UQ.

British Waterways –
Regional Office Midlands, 6th Floor, Auchinleck House, Broad Street, Five Ways, Birmingham, B15 1DL.

British Mountain Bike Federation, BMBF, 36 Rockingham Road, Kettering, Northants, NN16 8HG.